Gi-Ga-Stic!

100 Scottish Spooky Stories

A hundred haunting stories
of supernatural Scotland

Collected by George Forbes

LangSyne
PUBLISHING
WRITING *to* REMEMBER

Then my heart it grew ashen and sober
As the leaves that were crisp and sere -
As the leaves that were withering and sere;
And I cried: "It was surely October
On this very night of last year
That I journeyed - I journeyed down here! -
That I brought a dread burden down here -
On this night of all nights in the year,
Ah, what demon hath tempted me here?
Well I know, now, this dim lake of Auber -
This misty mid region of Weir -
Well I know, now, this dank tarn of Auber,
This ghoul-haunted woodland of Weir."

From *Ulalume* by Edgar Allan Poe.

Lang**Syne**
PUBLISHING
WRITING *to* REMEMBER

79 Main Street, Newtongrange,
Midlothian EH22 4NA
Tel: 0131 344 0414   Fax: 0845 075 6085
E-mail: info@lang-syne.co.uk
www.langsyneshop.co.uk

Design by Dorothy Meikle
Printed by Blissetts
© Lang Syne Publishers Ltd 2022

All rights reserved. No part of this publication may be reproduced, stored or introduced into a retrieval system, or transmitted in any form or by any means (electronic, mechanical, photocopying, recording or otherwise) without the prior written permission of Lang Syne Publishers Ltd.

ISBN 978-1-85217-647-1

Contents

An Invitaion To Fear 7
The Wolf on the Crag 8
The Lethal Tide 9
The Fairies' Dance 10
Unfinished Business 11
The Vengeful Mermaid 12
An Unwanted Visitor 14
The Clansmens' Revenge 15
Wounded By a Spectre 16
The Grey Dog 18
The Cutlery That Dripped Blood 19
The Helper In the Dark 20
The Grim Guardian 21
Buried Alive 23
The Floating Head 24
The Restless Bones 25
The Watcher On the Shore 27
The Kissing Ghost 28
The Restless Corpse 29
A Trumpet in the Night 31
The Wrong Turning 32
The Hindu Child 33
Heartbreak at Lovers' Leap 35

Mermen of the Minch ... 36
The Phantom Tattoo ... 38
Within a Magic Circle ... 39
The Perfumed Haunting ... 40
The Black Knight and the Scarlet Lady ... 42
The Cursed Clock ... 43
A Murderous Marriage ... 44
The Persistent Phantom ... 46
The Macabre Warning ... 47
The Skeleton Under the Stairs ... 49
The Grey Dog of Morar ... 51
The Lady in the Cavern ... 52
The Clash of Auchinyell ... 54
Creepy Corridors ... 55
The Face at the Window ... 56
The Snobbish Ghost ... 58
The Linton Worm ... 59
Murder Moss ... 61
Curtain Calls ... 62
The Annan Vampire ... 64
The Phantom Lorry ... 66
The Restless Reverend ... 67
The Head That Rolled ... 69
The Magic Mirror ... 70
The Disconsolate Stranger ... 72
The Dread Vision ... 73

Ghosts Galore!

The Well of the Bone...74
Sobbing in the Night..76
The Ghosts of Hoolet House...77
The Hungry Miller..78
The Headless Horror..80
The Beast With Five Fingers...81
Torn Apart..82
The Washing of the Shrouds..83
The Call of the Deep..84
The Strange Silhouette..85
The Haunted Brig...87
The Moonlit Lament..88
The Empty Grave...90
The Elder and The Devil...91
The Cursed Keg..93
Love For a Satyr...94
The Vision in the Snow...96
Footsteps On the Stairs...97
Corrie of the Goblins...98
The White Horseman..100
The Amorous Monk...101
The Devil Woman..102
The Wounded Deer..104
The Wonder Bell...105
The Cursed Mansion...106
The Hag On the Moors...108

Staked at the Crossroads	109
Dirges Over the Waters	111
The Black Hand	112
Home of the Ghouls	113
A Devil For the Women	114
The Galloping Lover	115
High Spirited Spectres	116
The Fatal Ford	118
The Fairies' Farewell	119
Black Duncan of the Castles	120
Skeletons in the Dark	121
A Dream House	123
Starving Spectres	124
Down in the Vaults	126
The Magic Herd	127
The Dog At Dusk	128
The Musical Cave	129
The Bloody Stair	130
The Housebound Wife	132
The Bogle of Bogandoran	133
The Robed Terror	135
The Dancing Vampires	136
The Doonie of Crichope Linn	138
The Ghillie Dhu	139
The Man From the Sea	141
The Searcher	142

An Invitation To Fear...

WELCOME to the uncanny realm of ghostly clansmen and spectral hounds, phantom monks and vengeful mermaids, the malicious wee folk and mobile coffins, green ladies and moaning banshees, restless wraiths and warning pipers, to those eerie regions where the afterlife and this world overlap.

The poet Dylan Thomas in the introduction to his collected poems recounted the story of a shepherd who within stone circles made ritual observances to the moon to protect his flock. Mocked for being "a damn fool", the shepherd replied, "I'd be a damn fool if I didn't!"

Likewise, these collected tales are taken from the allegedly truthful testimony of real witnesses to the events described. Whether they are objectively factual or not is entirely up to the reader's opinion but they are certainly based on facts.

Over many decades as a general news reporter in Scotland, I every so often encountered sincere, apparently honest and genuine people who described seeing apparitions of various kinds. Some of them talked openly about such macabre visitations but others were very reluctant – which roused my journalist's instinct that they really were perhaps witnesses to a true event or at least what they thought was true.

Anyway, there is nothing fictional or 'made up' about the contents of this dossier with regards to stated evidence garnered over centuries, so all we can do is put such incidents down to some more of life's great riddles. Maybe the old shepherd was right.

George Forbes.

The Wolf on the Crag

ON CERTAIN MOONLIT NIGHTS, a spectral wolf can be seen howling on the crag beside Stirling Castle. The story behind the apparition goes back to the 9th century when two Northumbrian princes seized much of central Scotland from the native inhabitants, Stirling being one of their strongholds which was guarded by hundreds of armed soldiers: but soon they too were under attack and efforts were made to take the town from them, just as they had seized it from the Scots.

On this occasion, it was the raiding Danes from the coast who were spreading terror.

At a crag on the southern side of Stirling, which was then little more than a collection of small, wooden houses built beside the fortress on the volcanic rock with a population of just under a thousand souls, sentries were posted to keep watch round the clock.

However, one of them fell asleep around midnight, just at the time when the enemy was poised to mount a surprise attack in the silvery darkness.

According to an old local chronicle written by monks years later, 'The besieging foe was at hand and was about to take the heights when a wolf, alarmed at the noise of the advancing hordes, crept for safety to the crag on which the sleeping soldier lay. But still the prowling animal found no peace in the restless darkness full of approaching men and growled loudly in terror and it was this baleful howl which saved the fortress for it awoke the sleeping sentinel who, realizing belatedly what was happening, raised the alarm.

'He was just in time. The citizens arose, buckled on their armour and drove the Danes from the district. Thus the wolf was the saviour of the town and fortress.'

It was later claimed that, in a fury, one of the Danes beheaded the trapped wolf in revenge.

The Lethal Tide

KINNAIRD HEAD CASTLE stood on a coastal promontory beside the Aberdeenshire fishing port of Fraserburgh until 1787 when a lighthouse was proposed and it was decided to utilise a tower as part of the structure.

Most of the castle was demolished as a result when it was adapted into this lighthouse but a haunted structure known as the Wine Tower still stands.

The castle was once owned in the late 16th century by the local laird, Sir Alexander Fraser, who first established the harbour and town below, though he bankrupted himself in the process.

Fraser had a daughter called Isobel who fell in love with a farmer her father deemed not good enough for her: but, despite paternal protestations, the romance carried on.

Fraser, ever a hot blooded character, decided to take drastic action. He kidnapped the farmer and dragged him to a cave beneath the Wine Tower where the captive was tied to a rock and left to face the incoming tide from the cold North Sea.

Fraser had planned simply to frighten this unwanted suitor as a warning and then release him but he miscalculated the ferocity of the high spring tide and the bound farmer drowned.

Isobel found out what had happened and ran to the cave where she discovered the lifeless body.

In a fit of desperate despair, she then flung herself from the top of the tower, killing herself on the jagged rocks far below.

Her plaintively wailing ghost still haunts the tower whenever there is a wild storm, as though she were searching for her doomed lover.

The Fairies' Dance

IN NOVEMBER, 1750, two travelling fiddlers wandered into Inverness in the hope of earning some cash in the taverns and streets but the town was quiet because of a sudden blizzard and they trudged across the old oak bridge over the River Ness where they bumped into an old bearded man who seemed to know them.

He stared into their eyes hypnotically and, enchanted, the fiddlers followed him as he said he was hiring them for a celebration and took them half way up the Hill of Tomnahurich where he began to stamp his foot on the turf.

Suddenly the fiddlers saw a large cave-like entrance leading to a brightly lit hall in which tables were laden with food and wine and a laughing, dancing company of revelers were carousing, all male and all dressed in green.

The awe-struck musicians were lavishly fed and drank deep, after which they entertained the merry company with a wide selection from their lively repertoire of reels and jigs and the night passed swiftly to the sound of lively music, jolly singing and animated chatter.

Eventually the strange old man returned to say it was nearing dawn and the entertainment had to end, so he escorted the fiddlers back towards the exit, giving them a purse of gold coins as payment. So generous was this reward that one of the fiddlers called down the blessing of God on the company – but at this the whole scene vanished and they found themselves back on the frost hardened hillside.

It was then that the fiddlers realised they had been entertaining the Sith or Wee Folk, Highland fairies with a great love of music and dancing.

Slowly the fiddlers wearily trudged back into town but then began to notice that an awful lot of changes had apparently been made overnight. The oak bridge had gone and been replaced with a stone one;

the buildings all looked different and the people were dressed oddly and spoke differently.

When they reached their own village, they found their contemporaries long dead and buried in the kirkyard and when they fled to the church the minister was just pronouncing a blessing on the congregation. At once the fiddlers crumpled into dust which was blown away by a breeze but their gold coins fell to the stone floor with a hollow, ringing echo.

For the festivities they had been attending had lasted a hundred years.

Unfinished Business

THE LIBRARY OF AN EDINBURGH MANSION, the property of a prominent Roman Catholic family, was reputed to be haunted, so the owner approached a priest and asked him to spend a night in the large room to observe if there was any phenomenon and suggest what should be done about it if there was.

The clerical watcher was ushered into the amply furnished, well stocked library and, with a supply of sandwiches and a thermos of tea, settled himself down into a cushioned armchair in front of a blazing fire.

He read a book for a while when, as the embers ebbed, he became sleepy. The temperature then began to fall dramatically so he drew his cape more tightly round his body.

Suddenly in the gloom he saw the pallid, expressionless face of a figure standing in a shadowy alcove and recognised a fellow Catholic cleric.

Summoning up his courage, the seated priest demanded of the figure what he wanted but there was no reply. Instead the ghostly cleric glided across the floor silently towards some bookshelves and pointed to a certain volume before turning his gaunt, white face pleadingly towards his interrogator.

Then he tapped the book several times with his long, bony finger. Finally, bowing as if in deference, he vanished.

The seated priest arose, walked over and took down the volume which the ghost had indicated. It was an innocuous enough title about Roman history but there was folded within the pages a thin sheet of paper with some writing on it.

One glance was enough to reveal that it was some form of written confession and the priest instinctively crumpled up the paper and flung it on the fire, watching until the flames totally consumed it as the dictates of his faith decreed when it came to other peoples' admissions, no doubt shown to another priest.

In the morning he related what had happened to the master of the house who told him the family used to have their own chaplain who took confession in the library. His uncle had been a deaf mute and wrote his down. Apparently one confession had been put away with a view to future destruction but for some reason this had never happened.

However, the spectre's religious duty now completed, the library was never haunted again.

The Vengeful Mermaid

IN THE MIDDLE of Loch Torridon, which stretches for 13 miles from the open, choppy waters of the Minch into the picturesque wilds of the western Highlands, lies a small, lonely island on which few people have landed (or have wished to land) over the centuries, known as 'Eilean-nan-Sithean' or 'the Fairy Isle'.

The natives on the mainland have never made use of its rich

pastures; and the local belief has been for a long time that it is an undesirable place to visit, being haunted by an evil spirit. At dusk, the winds wail eerily over the dark waters round the bleak isle's rocky shoreline.

This was an area once renowned for Merfolk, half human marine creatures feared by locals because such strange beasts, dwelling in caves deep in the watery depths, had weird powers that could capriciously wreak havoc on those they disliked.

Once there was a fisherman who came on a mermaid sporting in these waters. She had long, blonde, glistening hair and crystal blue eyes; and he became entranced when he saw her lolling on a boulder, combing her hair and singing her plaintive song in resonance with the low moaning of the wind.

Dazzled and enraptured, the fisherman loudly declared he was madly in love with her.

The two met regularly on the island but, with the passing of time, his passion cooled and the spell dwindled.

She was deeply hurt when he left her for another, a mortal in the shape of a local farm girl. The mermaid's love transformed into hatred and she plotted revenge.

One overcast day, as the fisherman sailed out alone to cast his nets, the mermaid caused the currents of the loch in which she swam to pull his little craft onto some jagged rocks and, as his boat smashed onto the island's treacherous shoreline and quickly broke up, watchers on the mainland saw the fisherman struggling in the swirling waters.

Then the mermaid surged up through the foam from the dark depths, clasped her gleaming arms round her victim's neck and pulled him down into the deep water.

He was never seen again and no body was recovered.

The strange thing about the deserted island after this tragic event was the heavy atmosphere of foreboding hanging over terrain devoid of wildlife.

An Unwanted Visitor

IT WAS ALMOST LIKE the script for an Ealing comedy when workmen threatened to go on strike over a ghostly manifestation. The problem occurred at the Royal Circus roadway in Edinburgh's New Town area when a large house was being divided into flats by developers in 1973.

They employed workmen to carry out the renovations but not long into their task these employees spotted a young woman wandering through the empty building.

She was wearing a long, white dress, almost like a ball gown or a wedding outfit, and was flitting distractedly from room to room.

The workmen thought she was just an inquisitive interloper having a nosey peek around the development and, when she was repeatedly spotted, they determined to have a strict word with her to explain that the building was not only private but also dangerous at that time: but whenever she was spotted they somehow could never quite catch up with her since, by the time they had downed tools, she had disappeared into the rooms and could not be found.

Matters came to a head one day when three workmen glimpsed her and followed her at the run to warn about this persistent trespassing. They succeeded in following the white figure into a room but repeated "hellos" brought no response. Then she apparently walked into a wall and completely vanished.

The unnerved workmen, usually so practical and cynical, were taken aback and consulted their trade union about the rules concerning ghosts, even threatening to go on strike, for apparently such a situation was not covered by any employment regulations.

After some heated negotiations and much head scratching, the property developers agreed to let a psychic medium, in the shape of a local priest, make an examination of the haunted house.

He did so and reported back that the woman was a friendly ghost who intended no harm to anyone, having died there many years previously. The renovations had apparently disturbed her rest but the priest undertook an exorcism ritual and the workmen were not troubled by any more visitations after that.

The Clansmens' Revenge

IN THE EARLY SUMMER of 1950, three old army comrades set out on a Highland tour with a caravan in tow and a car with a dinghy on the roof, eventually coming to a suitable camping site near Loch Dubh, four miles north of Ullapool.

The field in which they parked sloped gently down towards a cliff top above the loch and afforded fine views.

The next day dawned serenely and the men rowed across the loch and began to climb the ridge on the other side.

They scrambled over some loose rocks and disturbed the ground to such an extent that there was some subsidence.

Making their way down to the loch's edge, they were followed by a small landslide of boulders which they just managed to avoid.

However, they were surprised to find among the loosened rocks the remains of human bones and skulls. They had disturbed an ancient clan burial site.

In fact, there turned out to be so many remains scattered around the slopes that the travellers reckoned they must have disturbed the makeshift resting places of around 20 corpses; and they speculated that possibly the dead had been buried upright, shoulder to shoulder, as a mark of honour befitting military men, a custom found in other medieval mass burials.

As the twilight deepened and the air chilled suddenly, the

interlopers became distinctly uneasy with the unsettling atmosphere and quickly rowed back to their campsite, leaving the bones exposed as they had found them.

The sleeping arrangements involved one man being in the car, one in the caravan and one in a tent on the grass.

The evening was mild and calm but the tent dweller was disturbed by the sound of movement outside; and, on raising the flap, in the moonlight he was astonished to see the spectral figures of around 20 kilted Highlanders at attention in two ranks across the field.

The sleeper in the car had also been awakened and came running across. They both then hastily made their way to the caravan, shouting in alarm, for they saw that it had inexplicably started to move down the slope.

The two men raced helplessly after it and even hammered on the rear and rapidly retreating door but there was no response. They had to pull up as the caravan plunged over the edge of the cliff, dropping into the deep, still loch's waters where it splashed noisily then vanished.

Then they heard some harsh laughter behind them – but on turning round the field was empty.

It took days for the caravan and the body inside to be recovered.

Wounded By a Spectre

LORD ALISTAIR AND LADY FIONA were close siblings who belonged to a landed Perthshire family in the 17th century. Orphaned at an early age, they grew up intimately, almost as if they could read each others' thoughts.

Fiona married a local baronet and a few months later came down to breakfast looking pale and upset with a mysterious roll of ribbon tied tightly round her wrist.

Her husband asked her what was wrong and she replied that she expected news in the post that her brother had died two days previously at four in the afternoon.

Her husband dismissed this as just the result of a nightmare but shortly afterwards a maid did indeed come in with a letter bearing the tragic news.

Time passed and Lady Fiona went on to enjoy a long and happy marriage, having one son, before her husband eventually died.

She then became a bit of a recluse for a few years but out of the blue sent an invitation to two of her closest friends to join her at her castle for a few days.

Swearing them to keep quiet about what she was about to tell them, she revealed that she had not long to live and said that the night after he died her brother had appeared at her bedside during the night in spectral form, telling her he had been permitted to come back on a final visit as had once been solemnly agreed by a promise between them and went on to foretell that she would have a son who would marry his cousin, the brother's daughter, and that Fiona would die when she was aged forty seven.

As proof that this was not some kind of dream or delusion, Fiona requested that the ghost leave some kind of mark or scar on her that she would see in the morning.

The ghost then touched her wrist and it felt like being pierced by an icicle while the sinews shrunk up into dead scar tissue.

She was instructed that nobody must ever look at the mark on her wrist while she was alive.

After recounting this strange story and dismissing her baffled guests for the night, Fiona went to bed and was found dead there by a maid at dawn. Her Ladyship was aged forty seven.

The old ribbon was disentangled from her wrist and it was found the marked skin was withered.

A few years later her son married his cousin.

The Grey Dog

THE LONELY, WINDSWEPT AREA around Arisaig, seven miles south of Mallaig on the wild, west Highland coastline, is haunted by a phantom dog which prowls eerily over the heathery hills and through the gloomy woodland, howling plaintively.

Witnesses have described the apparition as being a large collie dog of a type once common in the neighbourhood which usually makes an appearance around sunset.

The sighting of its weird, pitch black silhouette against the red skyline, head raised to the emerging stars, often presages a sudden death.

The reason behind this haunting is said to date back to a period in the mid-18th century when there were severe losses among the sheep flocks grazing on the hills and the local shepherds were baffled as to the cause.

Victims were either found brutally savaged and half eaten or sometimes they had vanished altogether.

One day, a crofter's wife left her baby in a cradle outside her cottage and went off to fetch water, leaving her collie dog on the premises to keep guard: but on her return the cradle was empty and the bloodstained remains of her dead, savaged child lay on the ground. The dog was nowhere to be seen.

But on his return, her husband, met by his hysterical wife, went berserk with rage and, spotting his dog lying lazily in the distance licking its paws, savagely beat the howling animal to death with an axe and went on to destroy her litter of puppies.

However, the very next day it was discovered that a large wildcat, which had been lurking in the neighbourhood, had shreds of the dead baby's shawl in its lair and was in fact the real culprit.

The bones of some sheep were also found in the cat's burrow amid the bracken.

The discovery had only been made by chance when a farmer was roaming the moorlands looking for one of his lost flock. The cat was soon hunted down by dogs and torn apart and thereafter the sheep were able to graze in peace.

The phantom dog, known locally as "An Cu Glas' or the grey dog, is reputed to be that of the innocent collie, despairing at the impulsive violence of his master.

The Cutlery That Dripped Blood

A FEW MILES SOUTH OF STORNOWAY on the island of Lewis and beside a lonely moorland road that snakes its way to the village of Grimshader, there used to be regularly spotted the ghostly figure of a young man who would try to accost passers-by as if desperately wanting to tell them something.

These travellers always took to their heels so that the phantom never managed to find himself a listener.

However, this manifestation ended when a skeleton was unearthed on Arnish Moor during routine farm work beside the road.

It was of a teenage male and the clothing was dated to around 1700. The skull was fractured as if he had been hit with a heavy object.

The local tradition related how two youths, supposed to be attending school at Stornoway, went instead to the moors on an expedition to steal eggs from birds' nests.

They quarrelled when sharing out their spoils and one of them felled the other with a blow on the head with a stone he had picked up in the heat of the moment from the peatland on which they stood.

In a panic when he realised his companion had been killed, the assailant hastily buried the body where he had fallen and then fled the scene, eventually going to sea.

Years passed and the murderer felt it safe enough to pay his native Stornoway a passing visit when his ship happened to call in there.

On entering a waterfront tavern, the killer ordered a meal and, while waiting, noticed that the cutlery on the table was of an unusual bone design. On inquiring what the implements were made of, he was told they came from sheep bones found on Arnish Moor.

When his hands touched the handles of the knife and fork, the white carved bone began to bleed redly, spreading a scarlet stain over the wooden table.

The sailor started up, screaming in terror, and fled into the night and when he was later found, cowering behind a stone dyke, confessed to the killing, the words spilling out in a hysterical flow.

Although the corpse of his victim was not recovered at that time, nevertheless thanks to his own confession the killer was hanged on nearby Gallows Hill.

The spectre of his victim had been condemned for years to try and find someone to dig up his earthly remains and give him a proper Christian burial; and when this was eventually done then thankfully and at last the phantom by the roadside was laid to rest.

The Helper In the Dark

SCOTLAND WAS ONCE BLESSED with 'brownies', strange supernatural creatures of both sexes who were rarely seen since they only put in an appearance at dead of night when they would carry out manual or domestic chores for the owner of a house they had somehow taken a fancy to.

They were benign, helpful spirits but highly sensitive since they could not stand any kind of criticism and, if such carping arose, their services were likely to be withdrawn as abruptly as they were offered.

They also had a revulsion about being seen going about their self-imposed, nocturnal tasks.

One typical example haunted Cranshaws Tower which stands on the side of one of the Lammermuir Hills in East Lothian in the remote vale bisected by the Whiteadder Water.

The brownie at Cranshaws only appeared at harvest time when the cornfields were cut and the sheaves left in stacks, awaiting gathering.

During the night the corn would mysteriously be threshed and winnowed, ready to be stored for the winter.

This took place over many years and the owners were happy with the arrangement.

However, eventually a servant in the tower made the unguarded remark that he was annoyed the corn had not been stacked as neatly as usual.

The brownie, hiding in a darkened corner, overheard this adverse comment and was duly incensed at the criticism.

Deciding, as was the way with his type, that he would never come back again, he vented his anger by throwing the already gathered sheaves into the Whiteadder Water at a spot two miles from the tower, known as the Raven's Craig; and his services were never again offered or indeed requested.

The Grim Guardian

ABOUT THREE MILES FROM DINGWALL in Easter Ross there used to stand an old stone mansion haunted by the ghost of a workman. He had been part of the building force who constructed the house using huge chiseled boulders from a nearby quarry in the mid-

17th century; and he was killed when a large block of stone fell on him in a cellar at the bottom of the basement stairs.

In keeping with a superstition still prevalent at the time, his corpse was buried under the foundations of the mansion as a sacrifice to the old pagan gods whose rule had not entirely died out in this untamed part of the northern country.

In fact, before construction had even started, venerable local worthies had warned that this stretch of wild moorland had once been the site of ancient rituals during which demonic forces had been aroused.

After his interment, the workman's large, shambling, grey spectre was regularly spotted mournfully patrolling the area where he was killed as if grimly warding off invisible evil spirits: but his ghost was never seen on half a dozen nights of the year – at New Year's Eve, Midsummer Night, the Spring and Autumn solstices, All Hallows Eve and on the anniversary of his death which had been in mid-August.

Anyone sleeping in the mansion on these nights experienced weird sensations, one of them describing them thus, "Ghosts are not supposed to attack one physically but I dreaded that such an assault was imminent late at night in bed. It involved a sort of muscular paralysis and I could not breathe properly. A feeling of horror enveloped me and I firmly closed my eyes so that I could not see the devils. The temperature dropped but I managed to get to the floor, kneel and recite aloud the Lord's Prayer which seemed to dissipate whatever was there.

"My guess is the ghost of the workman acted as some kind of guardian, keeping the demons at bay and, when his reassuring spectre was absent, the hellish forces were allowed free reign."

The situation got so bad that no-one could sleep in the mansion on the six nights in question and eventually nobody would live there at all. The building declined into a ruin with the moorland assuming its ancient, gloomy aspect after the mansion's stones were filched to build dykes throughout the county. When the mansion vanished, the ghost of the workman also disappeared and people duly left the spot alone, just in case.

Buried Alive

IN THE MID-18TH CENTURY, an aristocratic woman in the Vale of Strathmore near Forfar was engaged to a local farmer called Edmund Graeme.

For his part, he was madly in love: but she was of a more flirtatious nature and, a few months into the engagement and feeling an oppressiveness and boredom with the marital arrangements, she began a brief but enthusiastic affair with another farmer on her land.

Meanwhile, Graeme set about making wedding arrangements: but then his morale was shattered when a friend told him what his flighty fiancee had been up to.

Thereafter, Graeme simply wasted away and his depressed body seemed too weak to fight off any infection during the long, bitter winter.

He died from pneumonia before the spring and locals were convinced the cause of death had really been his broken heart.

The same friend who had told Graeme of his fiancee's unfaithfulness now informed her how depressed Graeme had become when the bitter news had been broken to him.

In turn, she was broken with remorse for her reckless actions.

She gave strict instructions to her servants that her dead fiance's corpse was to be carried in a large, double coffin with room for two bodies, specially constructed by the local undertaker, and laid to rest in a quiet grove of trees which had been their favourite rendezvous.

The servants dutifully arrived with their doleful burden at the ordered time of midnight and laboriously unloaded the large, unwieldy coffin off a cart onto the grass and awaited their mistress's arrival.

Minutes later, she appeared from behind a tree, wearing a pale shroud.

Climbing into the coffin to lie beside her dead fiance, who she held in a last embrace, she then ordered her servants to nail down the lid and put them both in the large grave which had been dug. The servants obeyed.

But the woman did not rest in peace, for weeks later her grey phantom was seen by various eye witnesses flitting through the woods and she was in the habit of materialising before young ladies out walking on their own, always urgently whispering the same sad message, "Never be unfaithful to the one you love!"

The Floating Head

A MARRIED COUPLE ON A WALKING TOUR arrived at an inn near the Perth Road, Dundee, in 1880 and were charmed by its old world atmosphere, even though there seemed to be no available accommodation.

However, the landlord had a quiet discussion with his wife and offered the couple a room at the end of a long, shadowy passage which led to the rear of the building.

It was a quaint, oak beamed room with a big, ebony four poster bed set in a recess, while a deep and dark cupboard was let into the wall directly opposite.

The tired couple retired to bed after a refreshing supper: but the wife was awoken by a nearby church tower bell striking midnight.

For some inexplicable reason she felt drawn to the cupboard as if some invisible force was pulling her and instructing her in a whispering voice to open the doors. Almost against her will, she rose and did so.

The room was then filled with an unearthly red glow and a human head materialised and began levitating up into the air.

The woman screamed and staggered back to the bed, followed by the glowering head. Her husband awoke, startled, and then lay terrified as the disembodied and furious looking head hovered above them. He managed to stretch out his hand to the floor, grasping his walking stick that lay there and then swung it ferociously at the head – but it just seemed to pass through thin air and the head, untouched, continued to glare down at them.

The features were those of a red-haired, middle-aged man which then descended and passed right through them, seemingly going down through the floorboards.

The couple managed to raise the landlord and demanded an explanation.

At first he was reluctant to offer any and tried to convince them it had only been a nightmare but they insisted the room was haunted and he eventually admitted this and added, "What am I to do? I can't shut the place down. I have a 20 year lease and, after all, only occasional visitors are disturbed by the apparition. The head is that of a pedlar murdered and robbed a century ago, the body being hidden in the wall and his severed head under the floorboards. His killers drowned when the ship they were fleeing on with their ill-gotten gains sank in the Firth of Tay. Ever since, the phantom head has never been at peace. Apparently it is sadly unaware that his murderers themselves came to a grim end shortly after the deed."

The Restless Bones

ONE SPRING EVENING IN 1901 beside the small kirk of Kiltarlity near Beauly, Inverness-shire, three ghostly figures, apparently in some distress and moving among the headstones in the graveyard, were seen by passing villagers.

They were the grey and anguished spectres of a young man accompanying a woman with a baby in her arms.

The ghosts were regularly seen after that in the same kirkyard, usually at night but they retreated every time any human being approached them to investigate.

The local minister decided to look into the matter and one night waited behind a large gravestone in the ancient, tree shrouded kirkyard until long past midnight and his vigil was rewarded when he saw the luminous figures gliding past towards the rustling shadows of the willow-lined river bank.

They seemed to sense the minister's presence and the male spirit started pointing urgently towards the swirling, black waters of the river which was in spate.

This particular edge of the kirkyard was notorious for damage caused by flash floods in springtime and the torrential, seething waters often seeped over into the tombs.

On investigating the parish records, the minister found that a few weeks previously a small part of this section in the graveyard had been completely washed away by the river's flooding.

The ground affected had long contained three graves – those of a mother, a female baby who had died shortly after birth and the dead woman's husband, a woodcutter who had been fatally injured in an accident.

The following day the minister organised a search along the river's edge and soon piles of bones were recovered from the muddy banks and gruesomely piled up on the church porch.

The macabre task of disentangling the skeletal remains fell to the minister who found eventually that, as expected, he was handling the remnants of three bodies – a man, a woman and a baby.

When the search was finished, a new funeral service was held and the bones given a proper Christian burial in a suitably drier part of the kirkyard. A gleaming new headstone was erected and paid for by local public subscription and from the time of the funeral onwards no spectres were seen in the quiet glades by the river.

The Watcher On the Shore

SANDWOOD BAY, SEVEN MILES SOUTH of Cape Wrath in Sutherland, is a long, wild arc of windswept sand dunes, picturesque in summer but bleakly desolate in winter.

The gaunt, walking figure of a ghostly, lonely seaman has regularly been seen haunting the rocky shoreline, and, when the apparition has vanished like the sighing wind, no traces of footsteps have ever been found on the sand.

On one occasion, two local fishermen were gathering driftwood when suddenly the bearded figure of a sailor, in uniformed jacket and maritime cap as if he were a captain, materialised from nowhere and the terrified men dropped their wood and fled.

Some time later a farmer from nearby Kinlochbervie was on the edge of the bay with some of his farmhands looking for stray sheep.

As darkness fell and a full moon came out, the farmer noticed the silhouette of a man standing on black rocks, gazing out to sea intently.

Thinking he was a local fisherman, the farmer approached for a chat then noticed the figure had the bearing of a sailor on watch. He picked his way over the rocks but then on looking up the figure had completely vanished.

Weeks later there was a terrible gale off the north east coast and an Irish vessel was driven onto the storm-lashed reefs of the bay.

A number of bodies were washed ashore and bizarrely one of them was recognised by the farmer as the figure who had been standing, gazing out to sea.

Weirdly, one theory suggested that the stocky figure with the thick, black beard was the spirit of the sailor waiting on the lookout during specific stormy nights for his own demise in a shipwreck.

Certainly his unnerving presence has been reported several times since, usually on stormy nights, though how he could have haunted the shore before he was even drowned has never been explained: but witnesses continue to testify that he restlessly wanders by the waves with a visage as fierce as the stormy bay and eyes as piercing as clear salt water which engender deep fear and an urge to flee in anyone who has the misfortune to see him, even though he seems much more intent on scanning the gale-lashed horizon than seeking any human encounter.

The Kissing Ghost

HALFWAY UP GLEN LYON in Perthshire, which is the longest glen in Scotland, stands the gaunt battlements of Meggernie Castle, approached by a two mile long avenue of lime trees.

This redoubtable fortress was held for two centuries by the Menzies clan and used to be haunted by what locals labelled 'the kissing ghost.'

However, the phantom lady's amorous advances struck terror in those on whom her fancy fell – because she had only half a body.

Her lower half was sometimes seen sitting in a nearby graveyard but the top wandered around the parapets, corridors and rooms of the spacious castle.

Supposedly she had been the wife of a Menzies chieftain who murdered her when he became enraged with her flirtatious ways with other members of his clan.

In a jealous, drunken rage one dark night, the ferocious chief beat her to death with his bare fists then hid her bloodied corpse in a closet until he could devise a way of accounting for her absence.

He put out a story that he and his wife were going abroad, shut up their apartments and planned on his return to say that she had died from a fever on the Continent.

But first he had to get rid of her body, so he sliced the corpse in two to make his work easier and carried the lower half to the nearby graveyard one night where he buried it.

He then returned for the other half but his gruesome task was never completed for next morning he was found dead at the entrance to a tower, apparently having slipped and split his skull on stone steps in the dark.

After that, the spectral, upper, unburied half of his wife's body was a frequent visitor to bedrooms in the castle, especially when male guests were in residence.

She took evident delight in waking them up with a kiss which apparently was quite an enjoyable experience, rather like the touch of a feather on the lips, until the recipients of this phantom's passion realised they could only see the top half of their amorous visitor who then tantalised and terrorised them by vanishing into the stone walls.

Sometime towards the end of the 19th century when repairs were being carried out, the old closet was opened and the skeletal remains of a female body, comprising a skull and shoulder blades, were discovered.

They were duly buried in the castle graveyard and given full Christian rites; and thereafter the slumber of guests remained undisturbed.

The Restless Corpse

ONE SPRING AFTERNOON IN 1869 a man called Mackay from the coastal parish of Farr in north east Sutherland went out to post a letter.

It was a sunny afternoon and his journey involved a good two mile hike to the rural post office across a bleak, windswept, bracken-covered hill fringed with a steep cliff on one side.

As Mackay jauntily strolled along and approached the main road, an unaccountable feeling of dread came over him then suddenly he was confronted by a man who lived in a neighbouring village but whose face and hands were coated with congealed blood. This apparition had materialised as if he had shot up from the ground and Mackay staggered back.

In a quavering voice, Mackay then asked the injured man what had happened to him but was waved off in a cursory fashion. Mackay noticed that one of the man's fingers appeared broken.

Then the strange form seemed to focus on him and said in a deep, hollow, sepulchral voice that he had left his mother's cottage two days previously, intending to visit friends in a hamlet over the hill and had taken a path along a rocky gorge to shorten his route but his foot had slipped on wet grass and he had fallen into a deep, dark chasm where he had lain ever since.

Once far away he had heard his mother's voice speaking to a neighbour who was cutting corn in an adjoining field and with a deep, sighing groan he lamented, "It was so sad to hear my own poor mother so near yet so far away. Oh, it was cruel to be left there so long."

A cold, icy wind then blew and, as Mackay blinked, the apparition vanished as quickly as it had appeared.

Eventually arriving at the post office, Mackay blurted out his story and a search party was formed.

After a few hours, the lifeless body of a local man was found at the bottom of a ravine where the apparition had indicated it would be. Mackay was able to identify the corpse as that of the man who had accosted him on the hill. The head was lethally gashed and the hands covered in congealed blood. The middle finger of the left hand was broken.

A Trumpet in the Night

WHEN ANDREW LAMMIE AND AGNES SMITH met, it was love at first sight. Sadly, however, for this 18th century couple, a happy marriage was not to be. Agnes was the daughter of a wealthy and proud local miller in rural north Aberdeenshire who wanted her to wed someone rich and influential.

Andrew was as poor as a church mouse and his job as foot soldier and trumpeter to the garrison based at Fyvie Castle, seven miles south east of Turriff, did not offer any prospect of future prosperity.

The miller forbade the couples' ardent courtship but the lovers continued to meet in secret.

Meantime, the jealous Laird of Fyvie stepped in to the dispute for he too had fallen for the miller's beautiful daughter, though she had deftly spurned his advances.

This was more than the arrogant Laird could take and he decided to hit back after hearing about the young lovers' secret trysts in a nearby leafy glen.

The Laird easily fabricated false charges of theft against Andrew and had him transported to a penal colony in the West Indies as a condemned slave.

Andrew survived and worked on a tropical plantation in wretched conditions but after a few years managed to escape by stolen boat and gradually made his tortuous way back to Scotland. Never a day had passed without the love of his life being in his thoughts.

Sadly, however, Agnes was not there when he came home. She had died of a broken heart during his long exile.

The strain of getting back, coupled with the long hours of backbreaking toil he had suffered over the years, had taken their toll on Andrew and the tragic news of his true love's demise undermined his will to continue.

A short time later he died but on his deathbed he cursed the Laird of Fyvie loud and clear in a resonant voice, swearing that a celebratory trumpet fanfare would sound every time one of the aristocrat's family was about to pass away.

The haunting of Fyvie Castle began a short time later and for many years afterwards the death of a family member was always preceded by a weird, phantom trumpet blast in the chilly stillness of the night. This was often heard by the ill person and invariably hastened their demise.

The Wrong Turning

FATHER JOHN MCDONALD was a curate in the Archdiocese of St Andrews in 1930 and, not long after his arrival at a parish in Fife, was summoned late one night to a sick call at a cottage in the rural hinterlands with which he was not yet familiar.

He dutifully cycled off in the dark (his usual mode of transport) and, when he came near to his destination, saw a young man standing in the middle of the road, indicating the way with the words, "Up there, Father, you are needed up there!"

McDonald could not be sure in the dark but, though the figure was bareheaded, he had the distinct impression that the young man was wearing a soldier's uniform.

On entering the humble abode as indicated, McDonald found an elderly woman alone, bedridden and apparently very ill; so he gave her all the spiritual comfort he could while making arrangements for a doctor to call as soon as possible.

The old woman was obviously relieved by his presence but asked how he had known about her.

"Didn't you send for me?"

"No, how could I? There was no one here to send and when I took this turn I immediately took to my bed."

"Is this not...?" and McDonald mentioned the address he had been given.

"No, no, that's a mile further on up the road."

"But the young man who..."

"There's no young man here."

Baffled, McDonald made his way to the other address where he was indeed expected to attend to a sick man.

The following morning he made his way back to the lonely old lady's cottage but on arrival found she had peacefully died an hour previously.

Neighbours had gathered but he could not find anyone who knew of the young man he described; and they said it was unlikely anyone would even have been out on the road in the middle of such a cold night.

Then one old woman spoke up, "She did have a son a long time ago but he ran away and joined the army and I think was killed on the Somme during the war, though his body was never found."

The Hindu Child

A HOTEL, NOW DEMOLISHED, in Aberdeen was the scene of a bizarre, ghostly manifestation at the end of the 19th century. A nurse was called in to look after one of the female guests who had been stricken with a strange malaise.

The hotel proprietor knew next to nothing about his mysterious guest except that she was an actress called Miss Vining and had spent some time in India which at that time was still part of the British Empire.

The nurse needed to be with her patient almost continuously but no sooner had she entered the bedroom than she became aware of a deep, inexplicable air of gloominess. And when she approached the sick, semi conscious woman the feeling the nurse received was of some invisible force trying to place itself between her and her recumbent patient.

Miss Vining was too ill to talk so the nurse settled down beside the bed to begin her vigil. Gradually she dozed off then awoke around midnight when to her astonishment there was a small, coloured, Hindu girl sitting in a chair on the other side of the bed.

Startled, the nurse rose to speak to the girl but the latter solemnly lifted her hand and motioned her back. Unable to help herself, the nurse remained rooted to the spot.

Then she became so overcome with the strain of fighting a strange inertia that had settled on her that she swooned back onto her chair.

When she later awoke, the child had vanished but the patient's condition had deteriorated and she was comatose and delirious with what looked like a tropical fever.

Having ascertained from the proprietor that there was no Indian girl resident in the hotel, the following night the nurse made sure the bedroom door was locked and settled down to watch over her patient who had rallied to a limited extent.

The nurse dozed off in the semi-darkness lit by a table lamp but was roused by a sob from Miss Vining and once again there was a coloured girl opposite and once more she was paralysed by a wave of her hand.

The patient became more fretful and delirious as the child stared angrily at her but the nurse remained transfixed to the spot. Then slowly the girl rose and moved towards the window and her face was now contorted in fear and there was a large, shadowy gap across her throat. At this, the nurse fainted.

She awoke to find her patient had died with one hand flung across her face which was contorted in a rictus of terror. The other hand grasped the counterpane with such a firm grip that it had to be forcibly removed.

After the burial, the nurse was asked by the proprietor to sort out the dead woman's things, among which was found a photograph of the little Hindu girl dressed in the same Indian clothes that she had worn in the bedroom manifestation. On the reverse of the picture were the jagged, scrawled words – 'Natalie. May God forgive me.'

The significance of these words died with Miss Vining but for years later, although the little girl never reappeared, the hotel was said to be haunted by the ghost of a distraught woman.

Heartbreak at Lovers' Leap

THE GHOST OF A BEAUTIFUL GIRL with long golden hair haunts the precincts of Glencorse Army Barracks near Penicuik in Midlothian. Her appearance dates from an incident in 1812 when a mansion called Greenlaw House stood on the site and which was used as a prison for French soldiers captured during the Napoleonic Wars.

However, the rules were quite relaxed and the Continental inmates were allowed a lot of freedom to roam the surrounding countryside as long as they were back within the mansion's walls by sundown.

They used to frequent the nearby picturesque woodlands and, inevitably, encountered local girls out on various errands.

Some of these surreptitious meetings blossomed into more serious romances for the country lassies took a fancy to many of the exotic, flamboyant prisoners who had been allowed to keep their sometimes garish uniforms, especially the swarthy, good looking officers: but for one couple all their dates had to be held in the strictest secrecy, for the girl's father had developed a particularly violent hatred of the French who belonged to the nation that had killed his brother during a battle in Spain.

But one summer evening he came upon his daughter locked in the embrace of a handsome Frenchman in the woods and was so furious he stabbed the prisoner to death with a dirk he always carried in his belt, later falsely claiming self defence.

Since the victim had been an enemy alien and his killer a respectable pillar of the community, no official action was taken over the incident.

The girl was locked in her room for days as a punishment by her father but was eventually released.

Three hours later, her body was found at the foot of a rocky gorge known locally thereafter as the Lovers' Leap.

The mournful suicide still sometimes returns on hazy summer evenings to the spot where she took her life, still searching vainly for the only man she ever loved in her short life.

Mermen of the Minch

THE FEROCIOUS 'BLUE MEN OF THE MINCH' have been seen chiefly in the waters of the choppy strait which separates Lewis from the Shiant Isles a few miles to the east.

This sound has become known as 'Sruth nam Fear Gorm' or 'the Sound of the Blue Men'. These supernatural creatures are reputed to be of human size but of superhuman strength and their swimming round this stretch of coastline often causes havoc in the cold currents.

As their name suggests, they are blue in colour with scaly skins, long faces and extensive, muscular arms.

Local sailors were terrified of them for centuries because they took great delight in attacking ships. On one occasion a vessel came across a blue coloured man apparently unconscious and drifting on the waters, though in fact it turned out the figure was only dozing. He was hauled on board and then, when it was realised what his true nature was, the fishermen bound him hand and foot with strong ropes so that it was impossible for him to get away.

However, several other blue men bobbed up in the waves alongside, calling in a plaintive wail to him. He then woke up, snapped the ropes as though they were made of straw and dived overboard, vanishing under the creamy, swirling waters.

On Tuesday, April 7th, 1953, a Wester Ross fisherman was sailing from Diabaig on Loch Torridon north by the fishing ground off the village of Gairloch when he saw what appeared to be the head of a corpse in the waters. He steered towards it and, when 20 yards off, was astonished to see the figure rise vertically out of the waves to waist level. This terrifying form had staring eyes, a long nose and straggly black hair and his scaly skin had a bluish hue. Suddenly he dived out of sight and vanished in the depths and the fisherman heard some plaintive wailing borne on the sea breezes.

Another ship was once moored off the same coastline, a few miles south east of the Shiant Isles, when a bluish coloured man was seen climbing up the anchor chain. In a panic, one of the crew fired a shotgun at the figure which let out an unearthly roar then splashed back into the sea. Other bellowing sounds were heard as if the wounded blue man had companions circling the boat but eventually their sound echoed away into the distance.

On another occasion, again off Gairloch, a fishing boat was out on the sea when a hairy blue hand rose out of the waters and grasped the wooden side, rocking the boat from side to side. The fisherman seized an axe and cut off the hand. Again there was an unearthly roar and the water turned scarlet.

The fishermen tried to grasp the slithery, severed hand as proof of what had happened but it too fell and vanished into the mysterious deep where so many secrets lay.

The Phantom Tattoo

EDINBURGH CASTLE, Scotland's premier tourist attraction, houses many ghosts which is hardly surprising considering the frequent melodramatic, historic clashes and violent incidents that have occurred there.

One of the most recent manifestations – the phantom has only been around for a couple of hundred years – is that of a sad faced piper who haunts a secret dungeon deep in the dark, stone depths of this ancient fortress.

The story behind his appearances began in the early 1800s when a tunnel was uncovered leading from the Palace of Holyrood to the castle.

The piper agreed to explore its mysterious darkness and was instructed to play an air on his pibroch so that workmen above could trace his progress but a few minutes later the distant, muffled, skirling music abruptly ceased – and the piper was never seen again.

Repeated explorations over the days ahead failed to uncover what had happened to him, so eventually the accursed tunnel was sealed up – but on certain misty nights the missing piper's plaintive playing can still be heard echoing from the bowels of the rock.

Then there is the phantom brigade of ghostly troops said to make their appearance on moonlit nights around midnight who were first heard by soldiers patrolling the walls and guarding against a threatened night-time attack by Oliver Cromwell's besieging forces.

Two sentries were convinced the defences had been stormed when they heard many marching feet and drums sounding while pipes skirled an old martial song.

They quickly summoned their commanding officer – a Colonel Dundas – but, by the time he had arrived, all was deathly quiet. Furiously he ordered that the baffled guards be themselves locked up and ordered others to take over the midnight watch but only a few minutes had passed when they too heard the same alarming sounds.

This time Dundas took over the watch himself, convinced his men were either mad or drunk: but he soon found out they were neither, for he was suddenly awakened from his dozing by strange drumbeats echoing through the darkness to the sound of stamping feet approaching, summoned by a rallying tune of clansmen played on bagpipes.

He dashed to the ramparts and checked the shadowy promenade below from where the sounds had been echoing – but it was empty and silent.

Within a Magic Circle

HOBKIRK CHURCH, built in the early 19th century, stands in remote Border country six miles south east of Hawick. It replaced an earlier church, the stone foundations of which can still be seen covered by low mounds of earth adjacent to it.

The Rev. Nicol Edgar was appointed minister of the old kirk in 1694 and 26 years passed peaceably enough with routine parish duties and weekly worship until reports began of a ghost being seen in the kirkyard flitting among the old gravestones.

The phantom was described as a tall stranger sporting a black bonnet and with a morose, mournful expression on his greying face.

The hauntings became so regular that the minister's daughters refused to go out after dark, so the Rev. Edgar decided to do something about it.

Despite his 62 years and snowy locks, he was made of sturdy stuff and one moonlit, frosty night sat down patiently on a flattened gravestone in the kirkyard with a big, heavy Bible clutched in his arms. As an added precaution, he drew a circle in the grass around him, a traditional method, more pagan than Christian, of keeping evil spirits at bay, using for the task a family heirloom – an old Highland claymore.

Around midnight, a gently swaying white mist slowly formed into the spectre of a scowling man who advanced but stopped short at the intimidating circle on the ground.

Holding his Bible before him for protection, the Rev. Edgar boldly demanded to know who the ghost was and the reply came in an eerie, echoing voice that he had been a cattle dealer from the far north travelling south with his herd.

The voice went on in the still, icy darkness, "Last Lammas nicht, while returnin' hame alone frae a fair where Ah had sold ma herd, Ah wis murdered and robbed. Ma body lies hidden up yonder oan the moor under an old oak an' until Ah get a proper Christian burial here in this kirkyard, which is ma due, Ah will continue tae come each night tae this parish in which Ah wis killed."

The ghost then wandered off slowly and dolefully into the dark in the direction of the distant moor.

Hours later in daylight the minister organised a search party up on the moor where the body of the murdered man was unearthed under some bracken beside an old oak tree which stood starkly alone on the skyline.

The corpse was carried down to the kirkyard, a fresh grave was dug and the Rev. Edgar personally conducted the funeral service over the dead man. Thereafter the sad ghost was no longer seen wandering among the weatherbeaten gravestones.

The Perfumed Haunting

THERE USED TO BE a two-storey house with adjoining wings on the outskirts of Ayr, full of ancient rooms and long, meandering corridors.

On one occasion a female visitor to the house was so taken by its ramshackle quaintness that she spent hours exploring all its shadowy nooks and crannies.

Outside, in a central courtyard at the foot of some ivy-covered walls, she came across a bed of white flowers.

She thought it unusual that there was absolutely no colouring at all in this garden as if it had all been drained from the blooms which gave the place a grey, almost shroud-like atmosphere more like a graveyard than a garden but shrugged off this uneasy feeling and proceeded down an old oak avenue and once more into the house.

The sun was setting redly but suddenly the quiet air was rent by a piercing scream. The visitor almost leapt out of her skin and whirled round but there was only silence and emptiness prevalent, though she did notice a sudden tang of sweet smelling violets and on looking out of the window she noticed that the garden which had been so pale and lacklustre was now a golden yellow glowing in the gloaming.

Then, as if on a badly lit stage, the landscape slowly faded in the dusk and, as she stared open mouthed, the sight of a furnished room replaced the garden.

A door opened and in walked a young girl, carrying a bouquet of violets, who suddenly stepped back with a look of horror on her face as if she had interrupted something horrible.

With that, the room vanished and the garden with the white flowers lay placidly in view again as though nothing had happened.

The next morning the visitor mentioned to her hosts what she had seen and was told that four decades earlier the nearest part of the present garden had been a room extension which had now been demolished. One evening as the sun set, the house was broken into by burglars who came in through a window in this room but they were interrupted by a young girl who had been picking flowers and unexpectedly entered.

In a panic, they strangled her to silence her screams and ever since then her manifestation had always been preceeded by a scent of violets.

The Black Knight and the Scarlet Lady

THE ANCIENT KEEP OF KILBRYDE CASTLE stands two miles north west of Dunblane in Perthshire and during medieval times was owned by Sir Malise Graham, notoriously known locally as the Black Knight because of his ferocious temper and supercilious, cynical ways with any woman he fancied.

However he made the mistake of setting his sights on the virtuous and beautiful Lady Anne Chisholm who he began to court in a more chivalric way, thinking this more suitable for one who lived in nearby Cromlix Castle which ensured she would also come in marriage with a wealthy dowry.

The pair often met in a shaded, secluded grove halfway along picturesque Kilbryde Glen.

For some reason, possibly because Sir Malise tried to force himself on her in his usual manner and had his advances rejected, a violent argument erupted between them with the berserk knight going into one of his homicidal rages, furiously stabbing his sweetheart to death with the dirk he kept in his belt as defence against his many enemies.

He quickly buried her beside the stream, for even an aristocrat would have difficulty explaining away murder, and when Lady Chisholm was reported missing he claimed ignorance of her disappearance.

The Chisholm family searched the glen for months but no trace of the missing woman was ever found but soon there were rumours of a pale spectral figure being seen there with golden hair stained scarlet.

The wraith seemed to beckon to anyone who encountered her but witnesses had all been too scared to find out what she wanted.

Sir Malise was killed in battle abroad and his gloomy castle eventually had a new owner who one evening was strolling in the glen when he saw the ghost of a pining lady. She indicated he should follow her and, as if in a spell, he went with the ghost down into a glade where she stopped and repeatedly pointed at a patch of ground beside the stream.

Then she vanished.

His curiosity roused, the following day in the cold light of dawn the new owner returned to the spot carrying a spade. He proceeded to dig where the spirit had indicated and within a few minutes had unearthed the skeleton of Lady Anne.

The body was taken away and, after a solemn Christian ceremony, was duly buried in the local parish cemetery. After that, the bloodstained ghost was never seen again.

The Cursed Clock

A FAMILY CALLED GORDON rented a second floor tenement flat in Buckingham Terrace, Edinburgh, towards the end of the 19th century but were regularly disturbed by banging sounds echoing from the rooms above during the night.

On complaining to their landlord, they were told that the top floor was actually empty and was only used as storage space for antique furniture.

Nevertheless, the sounds of moving furniture persisted and one night the family's teenage daughter Diana was disturbed enough to seize a candle and then courageously make her way upstairs.

Oddly enough a door to a room on the upper floor lay open and on entering she saw what appeared to be the dark figure of a man bending down over an old, dusty grandfather clock, feverishly working on some mechanism within the wooden casing that framed the timepiece like a coffin.

What froze Diana to the spot, however, was the fact that the figure appeared to be transparent for she could clearly see the workings of the clock through the phantom's diaphanous mistiness.

Fleeing downstairs, she awoke her parents, describing what she had seen and they agreed to terminate their lease on the property the next day.

Before the Gordons finally left, they decided to do some research in the local library and discovered that a drunken old sailor had once lived on the top floor of the tenement who regularly imbibed rum until he was in a stupor, on such occasions becoming notorious for his short, violent temper.

One stormy night his drink-sodden slumbers were interrupted by a baby crying next door, so he stormed into his neighbour's room and shook the baby until its breathing stopped. In a panic, he hastily tried to hide the tiny corpse in the casing of a grandfather clock.

However, it was no use and he stood trial for murder, was judged insane and ended his days in a lunatic asylum.

Thereafter, nobody wanted anything to do with the top flats or the cursed clock so that floor was left untenanted, except for the guilt-ridden spectre who kept returning to the scene of his crime in the middle of the night.

A Murderous Marriage

THE IMPOSING STRONGHOLD of Dunstaffnage Castle, four miles north of Oban in Argyll and perched on a rocky peninsula, has two ghosts.

The first manifestation came about when Sir John Stewart held the castle for his clan against all rivals in the 17th century: but time went on and he still had no legitimate male heirs, only three daughters liable to be married off to local landed Campbells.

However, Sir John, who became a widower, was determined that his castle should stay within the Stewart fiefdom, so he was reduced to only one alternative – to marry his servant girl mistress and recognise officially their son who was now 18 years old.

The wedding ceremony was duly arranged and on the day in question the aging groom left the safety of his stone keep's stout walls to walk the short distance to the clan chapel. Guests lined the grassy path, including disappointed, would-be inheritors that included his own brother.

Suddenly a dark, hooded form darted out and plunged a dagger three times into the astonished Sir John who collapsed to the ground, bleeding profusely.

The assassin then dashed into the screaming crowd and made his escape: but his victim insisted that the ceremony go ahead, even if it was the last thing he did, so the priest came running out of his chapel to officiate and after the brief ceremony was over, with the bride weeping profusely and the groom being helped to put a gold ring on her finger, the Stewart chieftain then died where he lay, his blood spreading over the ground he had fought so hard to keep.

Thereafter, his ghost walked the bridal path, bemoaning his cruel fate.

The killer was a MacDougall supposedly protesting about his clans' lands being stolen by the Stewarts years previously but also said to be involved in the plot were the Campbells and Sir John's brother, jealous of his kinsman's power.

Despite this hasty, bloodstained wedding, Sir John's plan did not succeed and the castle soon fell into the greedy grasp of local Campbell warlords.

The second Dunstaffnage ghost is a Green Lady with piercing eyes known as the Ell-Maid who made her spectral appearance to herald any important events in the rule of the resident Campbell family. If she was happy and laughing, they knew something pleasant, usually a birth or a marriage, was in store but if she was sad and weeping it meant a death or something equally unpleasant was due.

The castle fell into disuse after a destructive fire in the early 19th century (foretold by the Ell-Maid) and was partially rebuilt but the ghost still endured, regardless of mishaps.

The Persistent Phantom

WHERE THE SLUGGISH WATERS of the Whiteadder burn meet those of the Blackadder stands the old village of Allanton in verdant East Berwickshire, just a few miles north of the English border.

In the 17th century, Allanbank House beside the village was owned by the local arrogant and tyrannical Stuart clan whose chieftain, Sir Robert, seduced a French maidservant called Jean, taking her away with him to her native Paris for weeks of passion.

But he soon tired of her and one morning peremptorily bade her farewell, striding out of her distraught presence dismissively, saying he was returning to his native Scotland and slamming the door of his carriage, ordering the driver to whip the horses.

The bereft, heartbroken girl made the mistake of running after him and tried to open the door of his accelerating coach but the postilion hit her with his whip and she fell to the cobbles where the heavy wooden wheels of the vehicle rolled over her head, crushing and killing her.

Back at Allanbank, the cruel, heartless Sir Robert arrived home one autumn evening after his tragic sojourn abroad but, as he swaggeringly stepped down at his own gateway, he saw to his horror, perched high above on the stone archway, the bloodstained figure of Jean staring down at him with furious, piercing eyes.

He promptly fled back up the gravel drive, not having the courage to return to his home and pass its portals ever again.

He never recovered from the shock and died in his bed from heart failure within a year.

But Jean continued with her haunting and on one notable occasion no less than seven Berwickshire ministers tried to exorcise her – but to no avail.

Visitors to the house frequently saw her pathetic figure wandering on the driveway, usually at dusk, while others recorded hearing the mysterious rustling of an invisible silk dress in the corridors.

Allanbank House was demolished in the late 19th century but the ghost continued to haunt the site and on one occasion a local childrens' nurse had arranged to meet her boyfriend in the old orchard by moonlight. He arrived early and rushed towards a pale female figure gliding through the grass. As he embraced what he thought was his beloved in the dark, the form vanished into thin air with a flirtatious laugh and he fled in terror from the ruins.

Most of the good folk of Allanton got so used to the spectre of Jean that they simply passed her by with a nod of recognition which, however, was never returned.

The Macabre Warning

THE BATTLE OF KILLIECRANKIE took place on July 27th, 1689, when Government redcoats were routed by more than three thousand screaming, barefoot Jacobite Highlanders charging down a slope in a pass south of Pitlochry in central Perthshire, led by the charismatic John Graham of Claverhouse, Viscount Dundee.

On the eve of this ferocious clash, Dundee was trying to snatch some sleep in his tent when a tall, shadowy man's kilted figure, whose head was streaming with blood, appeared beside his camp bed and told him to get up and follow where he led.

Strangely unafraid, Dundee, startled awake, rubbed his eyes then concluded that nobody was there and it had just been a nightmare but again as he tried to slumber the bloodstained figure reappeared, pointed to his scarlet head and indicated outside. This time in exasperation Dundee did get up but once more the figure vanished and pulling open the flap it was ascertained from the guard there that nobody had entered the tent.

Again he tried to get some rest but for a third time the shade, obviously that of a wounded Highland chieftain, reappeared and this time intoned solemnly that he would meet Dundee in the Pass of Killiecrankie the following evening "when he passed over!"

After the grim, foreboding figure had vanished once more, Dundee, having given up any chance of sleep, got up in the dark, dressed, summoned his second in command and then discussed what it could all mean. It is from this trusty lieutenant that we get an eye witness account. They eventually decided to let the matter rest but that it would be as well not to tell any of the men about what had happened.

The following day, Dundee was uncharacteristically reluctant to descend on his enemies from the high ground where his followers stood, keen to enter the fray. He confided to his immediate staff that he wanted the setting sun to be shining in his enemies' eyes and eventually ordered the ferocious charge to begin late in the day when the Highlanders, as expected, swept all before them.

But at the moment of victory Dundee, riding and leading his men, was suddenly struck down by a fatal, chance bullet which hit him in the side and unhorsed him.

He died that night and without his inspiring leadership his troops deteriorated into a disorganised rabble, eventually melting back into their mountain fastnesses.

The Skeleton Under the Stairs

AN OLD TAVERN USED TO STAND in Victorian times on the south side of a mountain near Fettercairn in Kincardineshire and the Rev. James Rule, Chancellor of Edinburgh University, sought shelter there one stormy night while en route to Aberdeen.

However, the hostelry was full so the landlord suggested he stay in an empty house close by, though it did have "a bad reputation."

Undaunted by such superstitions, the fearless clergyman bedded down alone in the old, empty house, having lit a fire opposite his bed to warm the room, but an hour after falling asleep he was awakened by the startling sight of a spectral male figure, through whom he could see flames dancing, lighting a candle from the fire and gesturing to the Rev. Rule to follow him. Not surprisingly the minister was reluctant to leave the comparative safety of his bed but the ghost ominously placed a poker in the fire until it was red hot and then put it on the floor, pointing at the recumbent figure.

At this threatening gesture, the reverend gentleman climbed out of bed and then followed the phantom which led him silently down a flight of steps, at the foot of which it placed the candle on the floor then vanished.

In the morning the minister asked the landlord of the inn next door if he knew of anything that might explain the apparition but the response was total bafflement.

Undeterred, the Rev. Rule, convinced some wicked, violent deed lay behind the manifestation, decided to make his own investigations in the district and to this end spent a week going through old, dusty parish archives and, having made friends with the local clergy, announced he had been invited to be guest preacher at the local church on the coming Sunday.

His investigations had come to nothing but there was a larger than normal congregation packed into the small kirk that Sabbath to hear this especially gifted preacher and the Rev. Rule shrewdly decided to take as a subject for his sermon the terrifying effects of conscience and how ignoring it could lead to damnation.

It was a powerful sermon delivered with the Rev. Rule's usual passion and after the kirk had emptied and he had shaken dozens of hands, the minister noticed one lonely figure sitting hunched in the pews, an old man who slowly, wearily rose and shuffled towards him with tears in his eyes.

The parishioner blurted out that years previously he had helped build the house where the minister had been staying but during construction had been involved in a violent altercation with another workman which had come to blows and the other man had fallen and broken his neck on some stone steps.

Terrified that he might be executed for murder, the old man said he had buried the corpse at the foot of the stairs where it had fallen and later claimed his colleague, an Irish itinerant, had vanished from the area to get a labouring job elsewhere.

The Rev. Rule supervised the unearthing of the skeleton which was later buried in the kirkyard and after that the ghost was never seen again. The old man was jailed for manslaughter and perverting the course of justice.

The Grey Dog of Morar

OLD SANDY MCDONNELL was the boatman at the head of Loch Morar who regularly carried passengers up and down the dozen miles of the West Highland waterway in the 1930s, using a large motor launch at a time when transport was more rudimentary along these untamed shores.

One day, laden with half a dozen passengers, he noticed a large grey dog running around on Eilean Allmha, a small, gloomy, uninhabited isle covered with wild holly near Meoble village on the south side of the loch.

The animal did not bark or whine but seemed to be in some distress, running in and out of the low, unkempt scrub along the shoreline as if searching for something.

One of the passengers, a ghillie called McFarlane, warned in Gaelic that the isle was a 'droch aite' or evil place and added, "It is no use, we needn't trouble ourselves. There is no dog there. What we are seeing is a psychic warning."

Sure enough, after the boat landed on the isle's shore and a search was made, not a living thing was found. The strange dog had vanished without trace, even though the outcrop could be covered by a group in ten minutes.

On the way back up the loch, the old ferryman was downcast and repeated the legend that the ghost of a large grey dog always appeared on this isle shortly before a member of the local Gillies or MacDonnell clan was about to die.

And, as if in confirmation of this, old Sandy the ferryman died in his sleep of pneumonia a few weeks later.

The legend originated from the days of the First World War when a gamekeeper, Donald Gillies who was married to a MacDonnell girl, went off to join the army fighting on the Western Front in Flanders.

Somehow his favourite dog, a grey bitch, while out swimming in the loch, got stranded on Eilean Allmha and shortly afterwards, not wishing to return to the mainland which no longer had her master, gave birth to a litter of pups that grew up as wild and savage as wolves.

When Donald eventually returned after the Armistice, he rowed over to collect his dog, unaware that she had given birth to a wild family.

The bitch fawned on him as he stepped ashore but suddenly the grown pups, who had never seen a human being on their isle fastness before, burst out of the bushes and, thinking him aggressive to their mother, tore him to pieces, devouring his flesh. In despair, the bitch leapt into the loch and was drowned.

Ever since, it was said that the ghost of a demon dog manifested itself on the isle whenever a Gillies or a Macdonnell passed on.

The Lady in the Cavern

BALCONIE HOUSE NEAR EVANTON on the west shore of the Cromarty Firth stands near the dreaded Gorge of the Black Rock, two miles up the River Glass, a gloomy and sinister spot with an oppressive atmosphere and an evil reputation.

Grim, sheer cliffs ensure no daylight reaches its inaccessible caverns, while from far below comes the distant murmuring of a river and the hissing of a waterfall.

In 1670, the Laird of Balconie brought home a beautiful wife from his travels abroad who became obsessed with this dank gorge, spending hours there each day, just gazing into its infernal depths.

Gradually a change came over her and from being shy and reclusive she turned carefree and flirtatious, even dissolute and abandoned in a way which had the neighbourhood muttering about bewitchment.

One evening she took her maid to the gorge where a dark man in green clothing suddenly materialised out of nowhere and, taking the young Laird's wife by the hand, led her to the chasm's brink.

The maid was rooted to the spot as her mistress, with a backward glance of infinite sadness, untied household keys from her gown's belt and threw them behind her, striking a granite boulder (a mark which can still be seen).

After she had bent and picked up the keys, the maid looked for her mistress who had suddenly vanished. Then, breathlessly, the horrified servant ran back to Balconie House and poured out her story.

An extensive search was mounted but no trace of the missing woman was ever found.

Ten years later, a local fisherman, climbing down the gorge for a basket he had accidentally dropped, came across a damp cavern guarded by two huge but passive black dogs. They let him go by and beyond he saw his basket of fish on an iron table and on a chair beside it sat the long lost lady of Balconie House.

When the fisherman offered to take her home, she pointed to chains that fastened her ankles to the iron chair which in turn was chained to the rocky wall of the cavern.

She begged him to flee for his life before it was too late as the dogs were becoming restive. He needed no further urging and scrambled up the difficult, slippery cliff to safety.

Again a search was mounted and again nothing was found. Locals were even more convinced that the missing woman had sold her soul to the Devil; and sometimes at dusk a woman's sad sighing can still be heard, echoing up from the stony depths of the dark gorge.

The Clash of Auchinyell

IN THE 17TH CENTURY, the old Auchinyell district of Aberdeenshire stretched along the southern edge of the Deeside highway to Braemar; and was partly comprised of bleak and barren marshlands known locally as 'the Clash' where local and disparate bits of the countryside came contrastingly together, a stretch where nothing had ever been known to grow.

No traveller after sunset would dare to linger in this weird locality as it had a bad reputation and was said to be haunted by the sinister spectre of a huge, fierce, black wildcat.

The hauntings began following the violent death of an evil local nobleman called Menzies of Pitfodels who was known to practise the Satanic arts in his strange and solitary castle.

Among the bizarre rituals he was reputed to have carried out was the sacrifice of a black cat whose blood he solemnly drank during a Black Mass at which various demons from Hell were conjured up.

A few nights later this same aristocrat was riding home on his best steed past the Clash when suddenly the horse reared upwards in fright as a huge black wildcat sprang from a high shoulder of rock onto Menzies who fell screaming from his saddle, clutching his bloodstained throat.

As the horse frantically bolted home, the struggling nobleman on the ground tried to fend off the vicious feline but it continued to tear at him and within minutes Menzies lay dead and ripped apart.

The first his servants knew of the incident was when the terrified horse galloped into the echoing courtyard of his castle.

They began a search by torchlight and eventually found the mangled, bloodstained corpse of their master near the Clash, lying contorted with a look of wild terror on his face.

The footprints of a huge cat were found on the marshy ground and, though an extensive search was mounted to root out and kill the feline beast, no other trace of it was ever found. Locals declared that no wildcats had ever roamed the marshlands but the screech of a large cat can still be heard on certain starless nights and its silhouette can be spotted bounding in the shadows beside the highway as if still looking for the aristocratic horseman.

After the death of Menzies, his Pitfodels estate fell into decay and the castle was eventually demolished so that the large, square stones could be used in the building of dykes and cottages in the neighbourhood. This collapse in fortune was said to be a judgement on the nobleman for consorting with the Devil and his creatures.

Creepy Corridors

HOSPITALS, WITH THEIR DAILY DEALINGS with death and despair, might seem a natural habitat for ghosts yet there are not that many reports of manifestations.

In Glasgow, for instance, there are only three well attested hauntings.

The city's Western Infirmary has a distinguished ghost in the spectral form of Sir William MacEwen, a renowned neuro surgeon who died in 1924.

Towards the end of his long and distinguished career, he was asked to perform an operation on a young local artist who was suffering from severe migraine headaches.

Feeling himself under pressure at the time (overwork in hospitals is nothing new), the surgeon, who was in his mid-70s, refused to perform the operation and, as a result, the painter, who was stunned that help would not be immediately available despite his excruciating agonies, leapt down a stairwell and was killed instantly.

Crippled by remorse, MacEwen died a few weeks later and many people have testified since that they have seen his mournful spirit standing in the corridor outside the operating theatre where he used to work, as if now belatedly keen to perform the operation he had turned down.

The former Royal Infirmary, now luxury apartments, had a ghost known as the Green Lady, a nurse who was killed when she tried to restrain a hysterical patient and fell over bannisters then down some stairs.

Over the years medical staff saw her ghost in the surgical block, appearing at various times, night or day, and ever willing to help any patient in distress.

The old Gartloch Hospital on the city's east side also used to be haunted by a woman but this one was reputed to be a matron from the days when the establishment was first opened. She used to glide along corridors and had the disconcerting habit of vanishing through a boarded up doorway.

The more ancient hospitals have spooky basements and shadowy tunnels leading to deep cellars (the Royal was built beside a medieval plague pit); and it is a regular routine for porters and even nursing staff to give new workers the fright of their lives by lying prone under a sheet in the mortuary, only to rise with a loud groan as some naive nurse passes by.

The Face at the Window

THE VILLAGE OF FEARN lies four miles south east of Tain in Ross and Cromarty; and, in the mid-18th century, an adulterous local farmer buried his shrew of a wife who had died of pneumonia and that same evening he called on a local girl with whom he had been having a long and passionate affair.

She happened to live in a cottage adjoining the graveyard and around midnight the pair were kissing and cuddling on a carpet in front of a roaring fire when the girl's mother happened to come in and caught them in mid-embrace.

She berated the pair and reminded the farmer that he had just hours ago laid his wife in the ground nearby and that yesterday she had "still been warm with life!"

The farmer replied angrily, "No, she was never warm and now she is as cold as ice, for she was bitterly cold long before we put her to rest."

As he spoke he turned to the window and then went deathly pale for there in the rain-streaked, darkened glass pane was framed the glaring face of his dead wife. Both the girl and her mother saw the apparition at the same time and screamed in terror.

The farmer fled the house and took to his bed, dying of a fever less than a fortnight later. It was said thereafter that widowers in the area took their time before they started courting potential replacements for their wives for fear of the wrath of their deceased spouses being visited upon them.

In the same village and around the same time, another farmer had taken a second wife who loathed the two children who had resulted from his first marriage so much that during the cold winter nights she would put the girl and boy, aged seven and five respectively, to bed with just rags to cover their shivering bodies.

They clung together for warmth but, after a few nights of this ordeal, the new woman of the house found that a big wooden chest, kept under lock and key, had somehow been opened and proper warm blankets put on the children so that they were able to sleep properly.

The stepmother beat them over this perceived bad behaviour, stoutly denied by the children, but every morning she found the chest had been opened again and the children tucked away cosily with proper bedding.

One night she kept a vigil in their room in a corner and in the moonlight quivered with fear as a door creaked open and the ghostly figure of their mother drifted in, opened the chest and tucked in her children with proper blankets.

Thereafter, the stepmother decided it would be more prudent to make sure the children had plenty of warm blankets.

The Snobbish Ghost

ARDBLAIR CASTLE stands a mile west of Blairgowrie deep in the verdant Perthshire hills, having been built in the 12th century on the foundations of an even older Pictish stronghold.

It belonged to the powerful local Blair aristocracy who were constantly feuding with neighbouring families, including the Herons and the Drummonds.

An old, rather imaginative poem tells of Lady Jean Drummond of Newton who was betrothed to a Blair as part of a fragile truce between the bitterly feuding clans but she was whisked away by a band of angry dwarves immediately after the marriage ceremony for, having no proper wedding dress, she had 'borrowed' green finery from some goblins without permission (green being their favourite, traditional colour) and so put herself under their power.

A more mundane account of her fate related that she had indeed loved a Blair but that this was thwarted in true *Romeo and Juliet* style because of the animosity between the two families and, as a result, Jean, overcome with despair, drowned herself in the nearby marshes.

Either way, her ghost is said to haunt Ardblair Castle and she can be seen most frequently on late sunny afternoons, sitting sadly on the window seat in the long gallery, gazing longingly out of the window and wrapped up in her inconsolable grief.

She seems a placid ghost and disturbs no-one because residents tend to leave her alone to her moping.

However, during the Second World War some rumbustious children from Glasgow's Gorbals district were evacuated to the castle, a state of affairs which apparently upset the ghost.

Instead of her usual calm if gloomy manifestations, she got up to all the tricks an apparition can perform to frighten mortals, like weeping and wailing, knocking over furniture and pursuing screaming figures along echoing corridors with outstretched arms and weird groans.

Her scare tactics worked because the terrified children tearfully insisted on being taken away from their haunted new lodgings and, having rid herself of these turbulent, lower working class interlopers, Jean resumed her tranquil seat at the window, gazing sadly out at the now tranquil scenery.

The Linton Worm

THE VILLAGE OF LINTON lies six miles south east of Kelso in the Borders and, on a stone lintel above the parish kirk door a carving depicts a knight on horseback attacking a huge, ferocious, serpent-like creature.

This commemorates a 16th century incident involving the notorious Linton Worm, a monster akin to a dragon with grey scales and a foul, smoky breath that lived in a cave on the side of Linton Hill near the Kale Water and which crawled out at night to devour cattle and sheep or any lost traveller who unwittingly crossed its foraging path.

The huge worm terrorised the area for years and, to protect their cattle, local farmers had to move their herds miles away but, undeterred, the slimy creature merely made longer nocturnal forays to devour its prey. Thus it grew bigger, stronger and more impudent, sometimes even being spotted during daylight hours lolling on a grassy hillside still known as Wormiston Brae.

Several daring attempts were mounted to kill the giant worm or at least to scare it away but the slithering reptile's thick skin meant that spears, arrows and stones merely bounced off so that it gained a reputation for supernatural supremacy.

News of the creature's depredations reached the ears of Sommerville of Lariston, a young and daring knight whose clan held lands nearby. He had been fighting abroad so was well trained in the martial arts and decided to face up to this worm as a challenge.

He scouted near the worm's lair and one moonlit night returned on horseback with a clod of peat stuck on his long lance and approached the creature's dark den, well aware that it would soon come out looking for food.

Sure enough, with a loud roar the reptile began inching its slimy way along the ground and, at Sommerville's urgent shout, his page lit the peat impaled on the uplifted spear and, when the worm opened its dripping jaws, the knight charged forward at the gallop and thrust his blazing weapon down the creature's long gullet. The lance was snapped by large fangs but the ploy had worked and, as agonised screeches echoed through the night air, the worm was burned to death as its insides blazed and then exploded.

Grateful farmers paid for the stone above the church door celebrating Sommerville's brave deed and the local minister gave a service of thanks that his parishioners had been saved from the attentions of this creature from Hell.

Sommerville was not only given a knighthood but was received at court where he lived out his days as Royal Falconer.

Murder Moss

THREE MILES EAST OF SELKIRK in the Borders lies a stretch of stagnant pools, reed bordered bogs and patches of soggy peat out of which a few old, gnarled alder trees twist grotesquely, a haunted, mist shrouded stretch known by locals as Murder Moss.

Its bad reputation stems from the mid-18th century when the area was frequently plagued by English raiders. One village which suffered repeated attacks was Bowden where lived wealthy farmer Davie Bonnington who, using his powers as informal feudal lord, had chosen a neighbour, known as Geordie o' the Mill, to wed his beautiful daughter Kirsty.

However, rather than the dour, morose, reclusive, middle aged Geordie, she was really in love with Will Hob who had left the village as a boy of 15 to make his way in the big outside world and hopefully gain a fortune which would help him return to claim her as his bride.

Geordie apparently showed no open resentment against Kirsty's amorous feelings for someone else but he was nevertheless missing on the eve of his wedding when noisy, drunken celebrations were taking place in the village. It was a stormy night and when the revelry was at its height there was suddenly heard the galloping hooves of English raiders and the party broke up as everyone fled back to protect their homes.

In the melee, Kirsty was astonished when her hand was grabbed by her true love Will who had returned hastily when he had been told the news of her impending nuptials.

He shouted for her to follow him and led Kirsty to his tethered horse, sweeping her up into the saddle and galloping into the darkened roadway.

Then the figure of Kirsty's would-be bridegroom, Geordie, appeared from the shadows on his horse, yelling, "Follow me. I know a good place to hide."

The three then disappeared into the dark and neither Kirsty nor Will were ever seen again.

In the days to come, after the raiders had retreated, villagers led search parties onto the moors where Geordie insisted he had left them safely but no traces of the couple or their horse were ever found.

However, months later Kirsty's white handkerchief was fished from a bog and suspicions fell on Geordie who was well acquainted with the treacherous quicksands in the area.

He became increasingly more morose and solitary, regularly riding out to the pools and marshes where one day he apparently just vanished.

Then the same lad who had found the handkerchief came stumbling incoherently into the village, pointing out to the bogs, and when a group followed him there they found Geordie's corpse up to his waist in mud, staring terrified through frozen, sightless eyes, his mouth open in a now silent scream, his arm stiff and still outstretched, pointing into the quicksands.

After that, vague phantom shapes were sometimes glimpsed in the marshes, especially at dusk, and the long, sad sigh of a broken hearted woman was regularly heard, wafted on the evening breeze.

Curtain Calls

MOST OLD SCOTTISH THEATRES have their cast of ghosts, the most flamboyant being at Edinburgh's Festival Theatre where the tall, dark figure of a professional magician called the Great Lafayette (real name Sigmund Neuberger) can sometimes be glimpsed glowering from dark corners.

He was last seen alive in 1911, running around the stage trying to shoot a terrified lion whose mane was burning after the building had been set ablaze by an electrical fault.

Investigators among the rubble of the old Empire Palace, as the theatre was called in those days, found nine burned bodies, including the double trapped in a box who the magician used in one of his tricks.

The Playhouse Theatre at the top of Leith Walk, which first opened in 1929, is haunted by a night watchman who committed suicide, an old man in a grey coat called Albert who has the mischievous habit of switching on lights, moving furniture (sometimes on stage during performances) and setting off security alarms.

The renowned actress Ellen Terry, at one time rumoured to be a lover of George Bernard Shaw, haunts the high balcony of the Royal Lyceum Theatre, wearing a long blue dress and viewing performances at one of her favourite venues. She was usually spotted by those on stage since the balcony, long unused by patrons, used to only contain lighting equipment. The distant sight of Ellen on high, staring critically down her pince-nez, discomfited many a performance.

The Citizens' Theatre in Glasgow's Gorbals is haunted by a Green Lady, possibly the spectre of a manageress who committed suicide by jumping from the upper circle.

Another female suicide haunts the Eden Court Theatre in Inverness but her tragic history is not connected with treading the boards. The theatre was built in 1976 on the site of an ancient bishop's palace and the Green Room was fashioned out of what used to be the old chapel.

The phantom which appears there is reputed to be the wife of a bishop who hung herself. Manifestations include mysterious footsteps and green mists, that being the colour most associated with ghosts because of its connections with the faery world of verdant woods and fields that give it a supernatural heritage.

However, it is a Grey Lady who haunts Perth Theatre in the High Street and she has the disconcerting habit of loudly putting down tip-up seats in the empty auditorium after the audience has left.

The Glasgow comedian Tommy Morgan, who died in 1958, still haunts the Pavilion Theatre in the city centre which he loved and where he was a regular big box office draw for decades. Suitably enough, his spirit has been seen propping up the bar or flitting along the corridors. In death he wanted to be part of his favourite venue and decreed in his will that his ashes be scattered over the roof of the theatre, a request duly carried out by close friends and fellow professionals.

The Annan Vampire

IN DUSTY, MID-14TH CENTURY CIVIC DOCUMENTS at Annan, Dumfriesshire, is recorded the well-attested case of a tall, dark haired stranger who arrived there from Yorkshire, at that time being ravaged by bubonic plague.

But, far from finding sanctuary on the long weary road north, it was soon obvious that the unwanted stranger had in fact the disease with him which was colloquially known as the Black Death, against which there was no known cure. He took up lodgings in a room at the local tavern but soon fell ill and died, displaying all the ghastly symptoms of the dreaded plague, so that he was quickly buried in the local kirkyard with as little ceremony as possible while his room was fumigated and bedclothes burnt.

However, during succeeding nights there were persistent rumours that he had been seen wandering in the dark, accompanied by a few vicious looking, spectral hounds.

The plague began to spread throughout the town and when the chieftain of the local feudal family, the Bruces who were related to King Robert the 1st, died from the unstoppable disease, it was decided, according to a superstition then prevalent at the time, that the

Yorkshireman should be dug up and his pestilential body completely destroyed.

At a heated meeting held in the town hall, nobody wanted to do the deed for fear of getting infected but then two brave, selfless young brothers, whose mother had died of the plague, volunteered; and, the following midnight, armed with flaming torches, a stake, a hammer, holy water and their weighty family Bible, the men crept among the gravestones and then began digging up the stranger's coffin.

On prising the lid open, they found to their horror that the corpse was swollen, the bloated face being a ruddy red, the mouth slack and showing pointed fangs dripping with gore. The eyes were only half closed as it the recumbent figure was only dozing.

One of the brothers hastily brought his spade down full force on the corpse's chest and a fountain of blood erupted and soaked the mens' clothes. The body obviously contained a lot more blood than a normal human being; and, as it writhed and screamed in agony, the two men hastily hammered a stake into its heart, all the while chanting special prayers meant to exorcise evil spirits.

The corpse was then dragged through the grass to a previously prepared pile of wood in an adjoining field where the bonfire was lit and the remains consumed by flames.

The brothers later claimed that they had heard a long, loud sigh of relief coming from the inferno; and after that the ravages of the Black Death ceased in the area.

The Phantom Lorry

A BUSY ROAD, winding among verdant hills dotted with grazing sheep and snaking farm tracks, links Stow village in Midlothian to Edinburgh; and along this thoroughfare a series of bizarre incidents occurred in the mid-20th century involving a mysterious lorry driving at a brisk speed and leading unwary motorists into peril along the winding roadway.

Witnesses in their cars and local residents, including shepherds on the hillsides, regularly reported seeing the phantom lorry driving silently along the former sheep track on Watherston Hill and then swerving onto the main road, the driver invariably being described as wicked looking with a diabolical grin on his leering face, while his vehicle was an old fashioned type from the 1920s, at that time not seen on the highways any more.

Its routine involved getting recklessly in front of one or two vehicles and careering along for a few miles before turning round a sudden bend and then vanishing into thin air over a grassy gorge.

The cars behind often followed and went off the road, plunging down an embankment because the drivers had thought they were following a normal vehicle over solid ground.

Fortunately, no one was ever killed but serious injuries were sustained. However, the situation became so bad that local traffic police stationed cars along the road where the phantom lorry was said to appear and on at least one occasion a squad car in pursuit of the mysterious vehicle almost plunged off the road through following it too closely, though the constable driving had been warned in advance about what might happen.

Various theories were put forward about the demonic driver in charge of the lorry, including that he was a phantom wreaking bizarre revenge on others still alive, using a stretch of road where he had been killed years previously during a blizzard which had blinded him when it came to driving. Such a fatal accident had actually occurred in January, 1922, but the details on it were now scarce. The phantom lorry had no identification marks to trace its possible history and no registration number, so any theories remained just that, without any proof.

The manifestation stopped as mysteriously as it had started and by the mid-1970s the phantom lorry was no longer being noted by motorists, though nobody could explain why it had vanished, apparently for good.

The Restless Reverend

AT GLEN LETHNOT IN ANGUS during the mid-18th century there lived an unconventional local minister called Dow who was notorious among his conservative and puritanical parishioners for what was considered his advanced and modern views.

When told that one of his flock, a farmer, had hung himself after a disastrous harvest, the Rev. Dow took umbrage at the suggestion that, as tradition maintained, the dead man should not be buried in consecrated ground since he had committed the mortal sin of self murder.

Insisting that the burial take place in his kirkyard, the bold minister sought to allay the superstitious fears of his parishioners by leaping three times over the open grave, thus according to tradition keeping the body in his grave until the Day of Judgement.

Nevertheless, the elders of the neighbourhood shook their grey heads in disapproval and maintained that no good would come of it.

Sure enough, a few hours after the funeral as darkness descended the minister was reading the Good Book by the fire in the upstairs study of his manse when he was distracted by a pale face with bloodshot malevolent eyes gazing at him, suspended in space among the flickering shadows.

The face floated out of the door, so, loudly commanding his maidservant in her quarters below to bring a candle and poker, Dow strode fearlessly onto the landing, only to be stopped by the sight of a huge, hissing black cat balanced precariously on the bannister railings.

Swiping at the creature, the minister only succeeded in losing his balance and toppled down the stairs, breaking his neck.

Dow was laid to rest in a grave within the kirkyard and years later, when the small church building was being rebuilt and extended, his coffin was dug up but, instead of being immediately re-interred in a new grave some way from the refurbishment, it was propped up against a low stone wall that surrounded the burial ground.

Apparently some of the local worthies had been having second thoughts about this unconventional cleric being buried among their nearest and dearest.

So the coffin, which was thankfully made of stout wood, stayed in its incongruous position for years since nobody wanted anything to do with it.

However, wear and tear due to bad weather meant that gaps appeared in the wood through which glimpses of the skeleton inside could be had, a gruesome fact which led to games and pranks among local children.

One of Dow's successors eventually ordered the remains carted off to a field and burned on a wooden pyre so that the ashes could then be scattered to the winds.

The Head That Rolled

ON THE OUTSKIRTS OF KILMARNOCK in an Ayrshire country park stands Dean Castle, a squat, medieval fortress which was the hereditary seat of the local Boyd family. They were brave patriots who fought alongside Wallace and Bruce in the wars against the English, continuing their military traditions by opposing Cromwell and his Roundheads and later by supporting the Jacobite rebellions.

By the fourth decade of the 18th century the castle was owned by William Boyd, Earl of Kilmarnock, an arch Jacobite who was quick to rally to the rebel colours of Bonnie Prince Charlie in August, 1745.

Boyd was rewarded by being made one of the Prince's privy councillors but while he was away soldiering his servants back at his castle reported a strange phenomenon. On several nights a phantom, decapitated head was sighted which appeared to have Boyd's features. It silently dropped through the air and rolled about on the castle's stone floor, while the eyes swiveled up into their sockets, showing only the whites. At the neck the spectral flesh appeared jagged and bloody. It seemed to have some kind of internal glow and vanished as quickly as it had appeared, leaving the servants terrified.

When this was passed on to Boyd who was campaigning near Carlisle, he mentioned it to his comrade, the Earl of Galloway, who grimly warned that it could be an omen that the Kilmarnock aristocrat would be beheaded at some point in the future.

However, Boyd laughed this off and maintained that the phenomenon must be that of an ancestor who had come to a grisly end.

After the defeat of the Jacobite forces at Culloden in 1746, Boyd, along with many others, had to flee for his life but was eventually captured by pursuing redcoats.

Taken to London for a show trial, he was condemned to the chopping block, the common fate of aristocratic rebels at the time.

As he stood before a gaping crowd, he told them about the omen predicting his execution and his last request was that his severed head be caught in a sheet since he had a fear of it rolling about in the mud. This was duly done.

The Magic Mirror

IN THE LATE 17TH CENTURY in Edinburgh, Lady Eleanor Campbell, youngest daughter of the Earl of Loudon, married James, 1st Viscount Primrose, who turned into a bad tempered, supercilious rake of considerable brutality, so that, after several years of domestic violence, the couple separated.

For the Viscount's part, dwindling funds and large debts may have had more to do with him fleeing abroad than any marital disharmony which he was in the habit of shrugging off.

He roamed abroad and for months Eleanor heard nothing about him until she chanced to meet a visiting stage magician who claimed he could locate the whereabouts of relatives, regardless of distance, for a small fee.

Hearing about his success with some friends, Eleanor went with her curiosity aroused to the professional fortune teller's temporary lodgings in the Canongate to inquire after her husband; and the alleged necromancer produced a large mirror which she was instructed to gaze into and which gradually became cloudy as if with mist. She then saw a panorama of a church where a marriage ceremony was in progress and was astonished to recognise her husband was the groom.

The ceremony had just began when a guest rose from the congregation and rushed towards the bridal pair, someone whom Eleanor recognised as her own brother. He looked angry and drew his sword, attacking the groom who sought to defend himself, whereupon the scene tantalisingly vanished.

Back home, Eleanor carefully wrote down an account of what she had seen, dated it then signed and sealed it in the presence of a witness, depositing the document in a box.

A month later her brother visited her, having returned from journeying abroad and she eagerly asked if he had heard anything about her errant husband and replied glumly that he never wished to hear this man's name again but related once only that he had met him under bizarre circumstances.

While staying in Amsterdam on business, the brother had become acquainted with a wealthy merchant whose beautiful daughter was heiress to a fortune. She was to marry a Scotsman of good standing who had moved to Holland. The brother was invited to the wedding as the merchant's guest but arrived late for the ceremony, though just in time to prevent the marriage of the innocent girl to his devious brother-in-law.

Recalling the mirror, Eleanor asked in trepidation the date of the encounter and then brought him an account of what she had seen which coincided in every detail with what had happened, including the day of the month and the dramatic circumstances of the abandoned wedding.

The brother was able to fill in the last detail – that the Viscount had thwarted his lunge, knocked him down and then made good his escape through the back of the church. Despite a pursuit, nobody knew what happened to the would-be bigamist and Lady Eleanor went to her grave not knowing the final fate of her husband.

The Disconsolate Stranger

TOWARDS THE END OF THE 18TH CENTURY, one of the still habitable wings of the once grand but now decaying Garleton Hill House near Haddington in East Lothian was occupied by the eccentric Miss Janet Hepburn, a tall, thin woman who stalked the countryside at all times of the day or night on rural hikes in a black cape, almost like a living ghost.

One morning, just before sunrise, she had seated herself on a hill when she was approached by a pale stranger with piercing eyes who seemed anxious to convey something to her but she was so alarmed by his sudden appearance that she waved her cane at him threateningly then stormed off home.

The following night she took care to bolt all her doors and windows and even put the key to the front door under her pillow but in the middle of the night she awoke to the inexplicable sound of the front door creaking open, followed by heavy footsteps climbing the steps to her room.

"Who's that?" she called out in alarm for, as far as she knew, she was the only person in the house.

Then unexpectedly the mysterious man she had encountered earlier loomed by her bedside.

"This was my home," the figure groaned sadly in a deep, hollow tone, "and I have a story to tell you."

But Miss Hepburn was certain he was a burglar and pointed to her jewel box, ordering him to take whatever he wanted and be gone.

However, he shook his head vigorously and insisted he only wanted to talk to her.

Terrified, she declared she would never listen to his tale and waved him away.

Then, without another word, the disconsolate stranger turned and left slowly, his footsteps echoing through the house until the front door slammed shut.

In the morning, Miss Hepburn was astonished to find nothing touched or missing, while the door remained bolted and the windows fastened.

She never saw the figure again, despite several sleepless nights, probably because she had declared in no uncertain terms that she wanted nothing to do with him.

The Dread Vision

ON THE WILD NORTH SHORE and not far from the mouth of Loch Broom in Ross and Cromarty, a solitary cottage once sheltered Sir George Mackenzie, an ardent Royalist busily engaged in raising troops in the Highlands to support King Charles II shortly before the successful restoration of the monarchy.

With some comrades he chanced to find himself stormbound beside the loch due to a severe blizzard and they desperately sought shelter in the lonely, lochside cottage where, after a while spent in chatting among themselves and with the friendly, sympathetic residents, Sir George's servant, an old Highlander reputed to have the gift of second sight or clairvoyance, went outside to attend to the small group's horses which were restlessly tethered in the swirling snow and neighing nervously.

On his return to the little front room and the heat of the fireplace, he paused and seemed startled for a moment before hurrying over to his master's side and urging him to rise from the chair he was occupying since he could see a dead man seated on the empty chair beside him. This was a sinister omen that could bring bad luck to anyone in the immediate vicinity.

Everyone in the room quickly rose, even though they could only see an empty chair which the Highlander was indicating.

The vision of the seated corpse was only granted to the old Highlander who described the spectre as a pitiful sight whose head was bandaged with a bloodstained cloth and whose ashen face slumped wearily while a seemingly broken arm hung at his side.

Next day, after Sir George and his men had departed, another group of horsemen was galloping along the steep side of a heather-clad hill nearby when one of the mounts stumbled, throwing its rider.

The man, badly injured by the fall, was carried unconscious to the cottage and was gently placed on the identical chair where the Highlander had seen his vision the previous day.

The unlucky rider's head was found to be deeply gashed and one of his arms was broken. A makeshift bandage was put round his wound but over the next few hours he succumbed to his fatal injuries.

The incident of the vision had been witnessed by some of those present who put their names to an account in a document later written up by Sir George who testified that the dread foretelling had proved all too true.

The Well of the Bone

COEFFIN CASTLE, now a picturesque ruin on the north west shore of Lismore Island off the Argyll coast, was not named after a funeral casket but took its title from a violent Norse prince and local pirate who was actually called Caifen and ruled his maritime domain from this formidable keep.

He came off fighting Viking stock and lived at the castle along with his beautiful sister who was called Beothail and who was as gentle as he was warlike.

At that time – the 11th century – much of the western seaboard of Scotland was controlled by Viking warriors who ruled locally in an extensive empire controlled from Norway.

Beothail eventually fell in love and became betrothed to a Scottish chieftain, an ally of the Vikings who was later killed in battle defending Norway.

When told the tragic news, Beothail pined away within a few weeks and following her death, allegedly from a broken heart, she was buried in a local kirkyard.

However, she did not rest in peace and her plaintive lamentations could distinctly be heard on the western sea breezes, wailing that she wanted to be buried alongside her lover in her native Norway.

Eventually, there was a response to her persistent manifestations and her body was disinterred, washed in a local holy well and taken on a voyage over to Norway where she was laid to rest as asked beside her lover.

However, her ghost continued to be restless and was seen regularly hovering over her grave and pointing to evidence of a missing bone in her left foot.

Again a longship was sent back to Argyll and eventually, deep down in the holy well, there was indeed found, after extensive searching, a small toe bone which had somehow become detached from the corpse in the washing process.

This bone was then placed in a small wooden box and taken back over to Norway where it was reburied beside Beothail's body so that she finally rested in peace.

On Lismore there is still a deep, vertical funnel for hauling up fresh water, now unused, called the Well of the Bone which commemorates this haunting.

Sobbing in the Night

PINK-STONED ETHIE CASTLE which stands near Lunan Bay, six miles north of Arbroath in Angus on the jagged North Sea coastline, used to be haunted by two ghosts.

The first was Cardinal David Beaton, a local religious leader who lived with his beautiful young mistress, Marion Ogilvy, and their eight children at Ethie which had been a fortress for centuries. He blatantly lived in sin, regardless of church law, for technicalities like celibacy and purity were totally ignored by the hedonistic prelate who loved the good life but ended up being savagely stabbed to death by conspirators at his other castle in St Andrews in May, 1546, during a period of violent religious disputes, his mutilated body being hung out of a high window on lurid display.

He had been persecuting Protestants and was responsible for the burning alive at the stake of local reformer George Wishart, so his own violent demise was not unexpected and indeed, for some, was more than deserved.

His restless phantom was seen haunting the dark, labyrinthine corridors of Ethie Castle shortly after his death, especially in the secret passage behind the wall of the room which was known as the Cardinal's chamber. His footsteps were also regularly heard and a portrait of the hypocritical church leader dominated the dining room for centuries.

An even older portion of the castle which dated from before the Cardinal's time lay unoccupied for centuries until a new governess arrived and spent a night there during the Victorian era.

She complained in the morning about being wakened during the night by the ghostly patter of a child's bare feet, by the heartbreaking sobs of a woman and the rattle of what seemed a wheeled toy somewhere over her head.

All of these phenomena reoccurred over several nights and

eventually efforts were made by workmen and staff to try and uncover the root cause of the weird manifestations.

It was found that the only entrance to the room above that occupied by the new governess had long ago been bricked up and panelled over.

When the wall was broken down, the tiny skeleton of a huddled, swaddled child in an old blanket was found beside the remnants of a small wooden cart which had obviously been used as a toy.

After the remains had been given a proper burial in a local kirkyard, the strange sounds in this wing of the castle ceased.

The Ghosts of Hoolet House

GLADHOUSE RESERVOIR in the Moorfoot Hills near Edinburgh now covers land where once stood Hoolet House, a farm-cum-mansion occupied by a morose, middle aged recluse who surprised his neighbours when he returned from the Falkirk Fair one day with a young bride.

The turnover of servants at the big house was regular due to the farmer's bad moods though one in particular, a young handsome Irishman, seemed to remain dedicated to his tasks.

But then the servant and the wife suddenly vanished along with £200 in coins which had been kept in an old chest under the landowner's spacious bed.

When no trace of them could be found it was assumed they had gone abroad.

Then, over the coming days, regular reports began circulating about the couple being seen hanging around the fields beside Hoolet House.

This became so commonplace that the environs of the house were deemed haunted and were avoided by locals, especially after nightfall.

Soon all the animals on the farm were stricken with a mysterious and fatal disease so that the farmer was unable to bury them all on his own and had to hire some hands to help.

These labourers had moved to a field to bury a horse when they heard the urgent shouts of the farmer in the distance telling them to stop what they were doing at once.

But it was too late – for a human hand had been uncovered pointing accusingly into the distance and the mutilated corpses of the farmer's wife and Irish servant were quickly uncovered. It appeared they had both been battered to death by a heavy spade or similar object.

The farmer fled before a proper investigation could be held into what had happened and he was never seen again.

The two corpses were reburied in proper graves in the local kirkyard and their ghosts were never seen again either.

Meanwhile, Hoolet House was demolished and its stones used to make dykes in the neighbourhood, while the fields were divided up among locals and the waters of the reservoir eventually covered everything.

The Hungry Miller

FIVE MILES NORTH WEST of the Glasgow Road beside a loop in the River Annan near the English border to the south once stood Jardine Hall, the ancestral seat of the local laird's family; and the rusty iron gates still lie deep in the long grass beside the ruins of an ancient tower where prisoners were once kept.

In the 17th century the local laird was Sir Alexander Jardine who had the feudal authority to maintain law and order in the neighbourhood and on one occasion he imprisoned a miller in the tower after the latter had set fire to a tenant's cottage over a territorial dispute.

The miller languished in the tower's dungeon, while Sir Alexander had to travel to Edinburgh on urgent estate business and unfortunately by mistake took the key to the prisoner's cell with him.

When the laird absentmindedly discovered his error, he dispatched the key back post haste by messenger on horseback but by this time a few weeks had elapsed and the neglected miller had died of starvation in the deep darkness.

Shortly afterwards, the Jardine household near the tower was plagued by the prisoner's ghost. A loud hammering of fists could be heard echoing from the dungeon door late at night which accompanied a pitiful voice yelling in terror.

Once, when the mischievous Jardine children poked a stick through the dungeon's keyhole, it was seized by something inside which then snarled in angry human tones at the intruders.

On the advice of the family's minister, it was found that, if an old Bible was left in a niche by the dungeon door, then the manifestation stopped but the book was eventually removed for binding and the haunting resumed.

The ghost even followed the Jardines to their new home where it came through the laird's bedroom wall, gliding across the room, complete with rattling chains, and out of the window, and such occurrences only stopped when the Bible was put permanently in the old cell which was never used to keep prisoners again.

The Headless Horror

BAUCHANS WERE IMMENSELY STRONG, squat, hairy creatures who could either be obsessively loyal or ruthlessly murderous, sometimes both at the same time.

One such supernatural beast was Coluinn the Headless in Morar who, as his name suggested, had no head and terrified all who encountered him on the stretch of road known as the Smooth Mile which wound down to a river.

At the same time he had an almost insane devotion to the aristocratic family at Morar House and would never harm any of them. In conjunction with this, the Smooth Mile was near to the big house and the Bauchan seemed to regard anyone on it late at night as some kind of intruder and any such traveller was likely to end their days as a mutilated corpse in a ditch.

One night the headless beast killed a stranger to Morar, a chieftain of the MacLeods of Raasay, an island off Skye, who had only been on a visit and had lost his way in the dark; and when the tragic news was carried back to Iain Garbh, the son of the murdered man, he set out for revenge and deliberately roamed the Smooth Mile late at night.

As expected, the headless Bauchan sprang out in front of him and the beast lunged with long, muscular arms, seeking to strangle the traveller.

However, Iain was alert and held the loathsome creature in a vice-like grip. He knew that if he could keep him like this for a couple of hours until dawn then the Bauchan would lose its powers in the sun's first rays and dwindle into dust.

As the eastern sky lightened, the beast struggled furiously and a sepulchral voice from deep inside the Bauchan's deformed, stooping figure (for of course he had no mouth) intoned that if he was let go he would never haunt this road again.

Iain insisted on the Bauchan solemnly swearing on bended knee which he did and just before sunrise the stooped creature was released and crept away into the bushes.

There was no more trouble on the Smooth Mile after that and Column the Headless went to haunt a peak in the western Highlands where, though a terrifying sight high up on the rocks to anyone passing by, he caused no harm.

The Beast With Five Fingers

ANCIENT PARTS of Edinburgh's Old Town, sometimes known as the Hidden City, lie deep down under the modern streets in a shadowy, complicated labyrinth of dusty passageways and cellars, many of them sealed off, and tourists thronging the busy thoroughfares above remain blissfully unaware of the sinister creatures which may be lurking below in the dark.

One such subterranean alley stretches the length of the Royal Mile from the towering castle to the more sedate Palace of Holyrood and is haunted by a phantom limb known simply as the Great Hand.

In medieval times this passageway was used in secret ploys by the garrison stationed up at the castle and could quietly be used to send troops clandestinely to the rear of besieging forces, after which the enemy would be taken totally by surprise in what looked like an enemy reinforcement deployment from behind.

It was a tactical trick which of course could only be used if the attackers were unaware of the underground route but, according to an old tradition, one officer leading his men through and then out of the tunnel was suddenly set upon by opposing forces who had been informed all about the ingenious trick and this man died in agony after having his sword hand severed.

Thereafter this passageway was reputedly haunted by the scuttling hand which behaved like a huge, leaping insect and grabbed by the throat those traversing the dark alleyway.

Several brave souls ventured into this gloom to test the veracity of such tales and their strangled bodies were later retrieved by armed bands with blazing torches which kept the menacing shadows at bay.

It was eventually decided to seal up the passageway and this was duly done: but it was never exorcised, so the ghostly, severed hand is probably still down there waiting patiently for any intruders.

Torn Apart

THERE ARE ARTHURIAN LEGENDS throughout the length of Britain with various sites claiming to be Camelot and other venues putting forward supposed connections with the chivalric tales of the legendary Round Table.

One of those traditions centred on the parish of Meigle in north east Perthshire near the River Isla, a tributary of the Tay, in Angus.

This story concerned Queen Vanora who was killed more than a thousand years ago and the Arthurian connection arises because her maiden name was Guinevere. She was the wife of King Arthur and the lover of Lancelot and the reason she allegedly ended up in an ancient tower on Tayside was because Modred, the villain of the sagas, kidnapped her.

He was King Arthur's nephew and ended up killing the regal hero in battle before succumbing to wounds himself.

Before that final, calamitous event, he had kidnapped Guinevere while Arthur was campaigning abroad and had taken her to his keep in Meigle but in turn was overwhelmed by Picts coming down from the north who stormed his castle.

Modred fled south but his fair prisoner was captured, still in her dungeon, by the victorious Picts who proved anything but magnanimous, taking her in chains to their stronghold, Dunbarre Castle on Barry Hill in nearby Alyth, where in revenge against the hated Modred they flung her into a pit of wild dogs where she was torn apart.

Her mangled corpse was then buried in Meigle kirkyard and ever since her pale, despairing wraith has been seen flitting among the stones, still dripping with blood and crying for help.

The Washing of the Shrouds

THE MUCH DREADED BEAN-NIGHE of Scottish folklore was a web-footed washerwoman who cleaned the phantom shrouds of those about to die, the latter sometimes being unwilling witnesses to her macabre actions.

She often carried out her grim task beside a river or at a lochside and, as she toiled away, sang a mournful lament whose keening pierced the air and the hearts of any passers by, bringing a searing sadness to all who were unfortunate enough to hear it, even if they were not the one about to die.

This is what any traveller would hear first, long before he saw the gruesome figure kneeling beside some stretch of water.

In some corners of the Highlands such spectres were often no bigger than children, though much older but in the likes of Perthshire they were stouter and clad in fairy green.

If a brave man managed to creep up behind her and capture her, she could grant three wishes for her freedom. Such men were then considered lucky but, if they failed to hold the bean-nighe and she escaped, then she could cast a vengeful spell that could paralyze limbs.

If the death foretold in the song was for himself, then the traveller might not let her go unless the wailing prisoner lifted her doom-laden prophecy and the march of mortality had been halted, at least temporarily.

The bean-nighe was the equivalent of the Irish banshee and is a particularly Celtic apparition commemorated in the lines, accredited to one such dreaded creature –

The banshee I with second sight,
Singing in the cold starlight,
I wash the death clothes, pure and white,
For Fergus More must die tonight.

The Call of the Deep

IN JUNE, 1939, while leisurely fishing from a boat on Loch Inchard in Sutherland, a lady staying on holiday at the Garbet Hotel in nearby Kinlochbervie suddenly noticed what she took to be a garland of rotting yellow seaweed rise to the surface of the water a few feet in front of the boat's prow, while the rowing boat was tranquilly drifting off Achriegill Bay.

Then to her astonishment the tangle turned round to reveal a beautiful, smiling, female face. The seaweed was in fact golden hair out of which peered pale, quizzical features with clear blue eyes and an impish smile.

When the lady finally managed to grab the attention of her dozing female companion, the mermaid had plunged from view, though her silver-scaled tail broke the surface with a splash before vanishing deep down into the depths, a sight which the lady's friend just managed to glimpse.

Back on shore, when the lady mentioned the incident to a ghillie, who had been helping her with her explorations of the area, he did not seem surprised and told her that this particular mermaid had often been seen sunning herself on rocks by the loch's shore.

This watery creature, although apparently friendly, had never actually spoken to anyone: but local folk were still afraid of her as something uncanny, an alien presence best avoided, especially if you were male and she had her lustful eyes on you.

It was rumoured that in the not too distant past such mermaids in the West Highlands and Islands had lured local fishermen to their watery doom by singing plaintively and longingly, just like the sirens of Greek legend or the Rhine maidens who combed their hair and sang enchanting songs on river rocks.

The mermaids off the Scottish coast so beguiled fishermen with their singing that it was not noticed that boats were being lured onto treacherous reefs and into dangerous currents.

A methodic search was later scientifically made of the area and some strange, inexplicable scales and fins were found in the fissures of lochside rocks but the hunt by so many humans may have frightened the maritime creatures off for in the postwar, more materialistic world their presence stopped being reported, perhaps because witnesses did not want to be accused of being mad or gullible or both.

The Strange Silhouette

AT THE BOTTOM OF A DEEP, MURKY POOL near Kildonan in Sutherland, a local tradition related that there lay a stash of gold. It had supposedly been hidden there by an ancient Pictish sorcerer who had also taken the precaution of placing a sinister guardian over the trove. This ominous sentinel took the demonic form of a huge, black, two-headed hound conjured up from Hell by the old black magician.

However, a sturdy local farmer in Victorian times was of a more practical bent and scoffed at such tall tales; and one day he decided to drain the murky pond and use the land retrieved for crops, duly setting about this task until there was a large, drying hole left in the muddy ground.

Since there was no phantom dog and no obvious treasure to guard, the farmer laughed derisively and, exhausted by his labours, trooped off home to an early bed.

Around midnight, the sudden hideous howling of a hound woke him with a start and, as he stood trembling in his nightgown and gazed out of his front window into the pale moonlight, he discerned in the shadows the distinct, starkly black silhouette of a large two-headed dog snarling and baying in his direction. He knew instinctively that if he opened the door then the creature would tear him to pieces and possibly even devour his limbs for disturbing its peaceful, timeless, ever watchful slumbers.

The howling echoed through the night air balefully, for there were two hounds' jaws baying for blood; and, terrified, the farmer cowered under his bed sheets, startled every so often by the mournful baying which however did not seem to come any closer, so that by dawn the two headed creature had apparently moved on.

But the manifestation continued for several sleepless nights and the farmer realised he would have to do something about it.

One morning he literally ran down to the hole he had drained and channeled nearby water to flow into it once more.

Only after this was done was he able to get a decent night's sleep and the phantom canine creature never returned, just as the farmer never laughed at the supernatural again and left the pool with its sinister guardian undisturbed.

The Haunted Brig

THE DROCHAID-MHOR or Big Bridge used to span the salmon-rich River Dionard near Durness in one of the bleakest straths that cut into Sutherland. When it was built, the techniques of bridge construction were only in their rudimentary development stages in the Highlands and it had a 'humphy-backit' style like many of the rural bridges of the time which meant there was a large arch upwards in the middle.

It was once haunted by mischievous goblins who could reveal themselves to certain chosen mortals with the gift of second sight; and late one stormy winter's night towards the end of the 18th century a mail coach driver was setting out with some heavy bags of letters but no passengers from the Durness Inn where he had been enjoying several draughts of ale since he had more than a dozen dreary miles of cold and windy road before him.

The gale and snow had a ferocious force that night and the next day some locals on the other side of the bridge were anxious because no mail had arrived as expected.

Several men volunteered to search for the coach which they reckoned might have been disabled in some way and as they approached the bridge a dark object was seen in the distance coming rapidly towards them.

This turned out to be a terrified horse that galloped past them but of his driver and the coach there was no sign.

But eventually the coach, overturned on its side, was found on the approach to the bridge with the semi-conscious body of the driver sprawled nearby on the snowy ground.

He was transported to his home where he died a few days later but not before he had told witnesses of being attacked by a malignant host of goblins on the bridge.

Swelling their ranks had been the ghosts of some men and women who had been drowned in the river over the years.

For some time afterwards, nobody could be induced to drive the mailcoach after nightfall along this stretch of lonely road. However, eventually a group of three men were persuaded to travel the distance involved as the brighter summer nights came in and the much calmer weather seemed to keep the demons at bay.

A local minister once related how at the bridge he had encountered during daylight hours and on a warm summer night a strange creature, tall and slender with a shroud all in white, who seemed to rise vertically from the river. It started to move towards him and he raced for the bridge, managing to cross it as he heard a scream of despair behind because the spectre realised it could not cross running water.

There were also reports of glowing, unearthly lights around this bridge before it was demolished during the Victorian age to make way for a more modern span over the dark, swirling waters which kept their own secrets.

The Moonlit Lament

IN THE EARLY 19TH CENTURY, a returning fishing vessel hit the rocks at Kylescu in Sutherland but her skipper, John Currie, managed to run her aground, thus saving his crew.

While waiting for repairs to be made, he became acquainted with a local laird's daughter, who had initially just come down to the shore to see what had happened, and their friendship blossomed into love.

Before Currie left Loch Glendhu for more distant ports, she promised to wait for him and he vowed to be true and marry her the next time his vessel came by. They also arranged that Currie would write to her regularly, no matter where he was.

Sir John Mackenzie of Achmore in Assynt was also seeking the girl's hand in marriage and, although she had no reciprocal feelings at all for the older aristocrat, her father was anxious she should marry such a man of rank and did his utmost to make her forget her seaman lover to the extent of intercepting adoring letters from Currie to his daughter.

She thus despaired of ever seeing her true love again and nightly sang a lament she had made up called *Black Haired Currie of the Rope* (which is still occasionally sung in the area).

Eventually she yielded to her father's persuasions and married Sir John: but a few months later Currie did indeed come back, only to be told the love of his life was married.

Furious and determined to prove that he at least had been faithful, Currie set out for Achmore and when Sir John saw him approach he fled to the hills, thus allowing the returning seaman to spend a few daylight hours with his former sweetheart which, however, turned into an angry confrontation with bitter recriminations flying between them, possibly as Sir John had intended.

As darkness fell, Currie then stormed off to the local tavern and drank himself into oblivion.

Staggering back to his vessel, the inebriated seaman did not see Sir John, who had realised his wife still loved Currie, despite all that had transpired, lurking in the bushes with a shotgun. Suddenly the aristocrat rose and blasted his rival through the heart, killing him instantly.

Minutes later, the body was dragged into a nearby loch and Sir John, by this time deranged, stalked home in a homicidal fury, turned the gun on his new wife and then on himself.

The ghost of the murdered skipper is still said to haunt the area and those who have passed Achmore late at night have declared they have seen the wraith of the distraught girl and have heard the strains of her plaintive voice singing, "Currie Dubh Nan Ropa..."

The Empty Grave

IN THE PARISH OF ALNESS in eastern Ross and Cromarty, three quarters of a mile north of the Black Rock of Novar, there lies an old kirk, surrounded by overgrown trees, beside which lies a derelict graveyard with some stone slabs embedded in the weed-ridden grass.

One of the stones was of particular interest to the smuggler Old Donald Fraser in the mid-18th century, for below the marker was no corpse but plenty of contraband brandy and wine barrels.

Donald's clandestine bothy, which served as a storage den for illicit spirits, was in the Black Rock, so well hidden that the redcoated and armed government excisemen, keen to enforce national taxation, never found it.

Donald used his rowing boat to offload barrels of spirits from Continental cargo vessels. As a lucrative sideline and also for personal use, he concocted his own moonshine whisky from a large still beside his bothy.

One midnight he was in the kirkyard pulling back the heavy gravestone when he noticed a shadowy silhouette nearby, watching him.

Fearing he had been caught by a customs man, the strange figure reassured him, "Fear not, Donald, for I am a man after your own heart."

"Who are you?"

"My name does not matter but it is few graves that I do not know about."

"You'll be a minister or a doctor then; and out for a bit of sport, just like myself?"

"Maybe, but what I want is for you to take me to your hidden bothy and let me see how you draw the whisky, for I hear you are easily the best in all the land at making such a wondrous drink."

Flattered, Donald now noticed more personal details about this stranger and that he was a tall, sallow, saturnine man with a long black cloak which reached almost to the ground and a red beret pulled down at a rakish angle over his head.

Donald ushered him to follow and then led him to his bothy in the undergrowth where a few of the smuggler's cronies had gathered. It was not long before the whisky started flowing which led to much merriment, including singing, dancing and wild laughing.

The stranger then rattled some coins in a dangling purse and bet how close they could jump to a cliff edge which towered over Loch Glass lying placidly far below.

Just as a staggering ghillie was about to make a reckless leap, swooping out of the shadows came a snow-white ptarmigan that had broken its wing and that Donald had nursed back to health.

It fluttered high around the company and gave a squawk like a moor fowl which to the assembled company seemed to sound like, "Go back! Go back!"

Suddenly the stranger rose, hissed sibilantly and transformed into what looked like a looming, bat-like creature which flew forwards over the cliff and down into the loch's depths with a loud splash where the water bubbled redly for a moment.

The carousers quickly sobered up on realising this had been a demon from Hell after their souls and they all fled the scene chaotically.

The Elder and The Devil

GLEN URQUHART, extending for seven miles from Loch Ness, despite its comparatively central position in the Highlands was once one of the most remote spots in the north and did not even have public transport reaching its doors until the 1920s.

The castle and its environs long had a doom laden atmosphere and a grim reputation which meant it was often avoided by travellers if possible, not least because it was reputed to be haunted by no less than three spectres, namely the Black, Speckled and White Devils.

One typical tale involving the first of these took place in 1900 when an elder of the local kirk was summoned to the side of a dying, bedridden shepherd to pray for his soul in a distant cottage.

It was a dark, stormy night but nevertheless, deeming it his Christian duty to attend, the elder wrapped himself up in a sturdy cloak and set out, tramping the long, winding, lonely road through the wind and rain.

As he passed along the shadowy, wooded bank of the Meikle Burn, the elder was astonished to hear the sound of whimpering between blasts of the gale and was even more surprised to trace the source of the sound to a baby in swaddling clothes lying under a gorse bush.

Quickly wrapping the shivering baby in the warmer, enveloping folds of his voluminous cloak, the elder hoisted the huddled form onto his back to make it easier to carry and, holding his burden firmly by the arms, continued on his way, head bent.

But gradually the load seemed to become heavier, his footsteps more faltering and fatiguing and eventually he felt there was need for some rest beside the roadway.

Then, after a few minutes recuperation and when he felt ready enough to press onwards, the elder was horrified to find he was being forced down by two hairy hands with talons where the baby should have been.

The elder sought to tear off the claws trying to strangle him and realised too late that the baby had been a demon in disguise.

He cried out in prayer, imploring God's help and suddenly the evil creature shrank and scuttled into the dark in despair with a cry of abject grief being carried on the icy wind.

The elder was now free to continue on his way which he did with a more sprightly step so that he was soon able to fulfill his mission of kneeling and praying with the old shepherd in his warm cottage, something the demon had obviously wanted to prevent.

The invalid died quietly during the wee' sma' hours but all through that long, sad night the elder could not be sure whether there was just a wind howling round the cottage or whether there was a more unearthly and malignant wailing involved.

Regardless, the elder deemed it more prudent to wait until daylight before returning to his village with the sad news and the tale of his terrible trip.

The Cursed Keg

TOWARDS THE END OF THE 19TH CENTURY there was a terrific storm in the waters off western Sutherland and several wrecks were cast along the creamy, rock strewn shoreline.

Among the debris washed ashore was a keg of whisky which ended up on the beach at Kerracher Bay in Loch Cairnbawn where it was discovered by an old, grizzled fisherman named Jamie Tordeas who laboriously carried the wooden cask into the ancient ferryhouse which also served as the local inn.

After depositing the keg in an upstairs room on the west side of the building where access could only be gained by a wooden loft ladder, Tordeas invited some of his cronies to come and share its contents one Saturday night.

During the drunken debacle which followed, one of those present, who claimed to be a seer with second sight, suddenly arose in the midst of the noisy festivities and declared solemnly that a great tragedy would take place that very night.

This dismal prophecy was ridiculed by the roistering revelers who just proceeded to get more drunk and after a while, as so often happens on these inebriated occasions, a heated argument started over next to nothing which became so loud that Tordeas had to protest that the hour of the holy Sabbath was fast approaching, the holy day so beloved of the Gaels when those present would have to wend their way home and sober up in time for the church sermon.

However, the son of Tordeas, a violent young man, was still in a bad mood and came to grips with his father, flinging him down the ladder.

The fall broke the old man's neck and he died in agony, screaming, "My son, I will return to have my revenge!"

A few weeks later vengeance did indeed strike home when the son's drowned body was found washed up on the shore of nearby Loch Glencoul with no explanation as to how he met this fate, though there was a look of terror frozen on his contorted features.

The ghost of Tordeas appears annually at midnight on the anniversary of his untimely death, just beneath the attic which has remained unused since the tragedy.

One of the witnesses to this apparition in the 1950s was Professor C.M. Joad, a resident at what was then the Kylescu Hotel, who was a popular member of the *Brains Trust*, a weekly radio programme on the old BBC Home Service.

Love For a Satyr

IN 1733 A BEAUTIFUL GIRL in Caithness incurred the wrath of a local 'wise woman' because she was much lovelier than the old witch who pronounced on her a gruesome guidhe or curse.

Like Titania, the Queen of the Fairies who in *A Midsummer Night's Dream* is deluded into loving a donkey, this was a spell which meant the girl was to love a monster: but she just laughed at the ugly old woman's declared malign enchantment and soon forgot all about it.

As the girl grew older, she decided to marry a prosperous farmer from Strathmore and on their wedding day he was bringing her from Strathhalladale to his cottage when a dense mist descended on them as they crossed a lonely moor.

They lost their way and came upon a deserted bothy where they sought shelter for the night; and, managing to light a fire, they were sitting silently by it when without warning a strange being entered who in his upper form was like a young man but who was also bearded, goat-faced, seemingly with furry legs and boasting the tail of a horse.

"Who is to have this woman?" asked this bizarre satyr in a booming voice.

"Who," the farmer boldly replied, "but he to whom she belongs!"

"Then let us fight for her!" declared the satyr.

The pair then joined and began to punch and tussle and, under the strong farmer's fierce, hard blows, the monster soon lay bruised and beaten on the earthen floor.

Then, to the farmer's astonishment, his new bride, who had been standing meekly in the background, now ran forward to help the stricken creature and actually turned on his assailant furiously.

Horror struck at her disloyalty but being unable to strike her, the farmer sadly realised his only alternative was flight and so headed home with a heavy heart.

After a few days his wife appeared at Strathmore, apparently cured of her enchanted infatuation: but in nine months time she gave birth to a son who resembled the monster's uncanny features more than her husband's.

This incident was recounted as authentic by Dr Alexander McBain in a paper delivered to the Gaelic Society of Inverness in 1888.

Descendants of the satyr were still supposed to be alive at that time and living near Bonar Bridge in Sutherland.

The Vision in the Snow

ON NEW YEAR'S EVE, 1923, a young shepherd walked from his croft the eight miles to the nearest hamlet, Oykell Bridge in Sutherland, to call on some friends and imbibe the traditional festive spirit.

He had a few drinks in good company then called later on at a farmer's house two miles up the glen where he spent a few convivial hours and brought in the New Year.

The countryside had been plagued with blizzards which made the roads difficult to traverse when they turned into sheets of ice, so folk on the move thought it more prudent if laborious to wade through the deeper snowdrifts in fields on the verges of treacherous thoroughfares.

Around ten o'clock the following day which dawned white and silent, a local farmer went out to feed his herd along with his 11-year-old son to help him; and on passing the gable of a shed they noticed the dark silhouette of the young shepherd in the snow drifts walking downhill in a stiff but resolute manner. They both remarked on his fast, incredibly sure footed walking despite the freezing conditions.

The shepherd strode out quickly towards the end of the road and the boy, rather curious, ran forward to see what fittings the shepherd had on his boots which gave him such confidence but on glancing upwards he noticed that the figure had completely vanished in the white vastness. Nor were there any footprints in the snow which lay silent and undisturbed all around.

Later in the day an alarming message arrived from the shepherd's croft to the effect that he had not come back from the previous night's celebrations.

A search was mounted and eventually his frozen corpse was found near some rocks where he had fallen and broken his leg.

The corpse was taken home and a doctor called who gave the time of death as roughly ten o'clock that morning, the same time at which his form had been seen striding down the snowbound hill.

Footsteps On the Stairs

A YOUNG WOMAN from Kinlochbervie was, during the first decade of the 20th century, a housekeeper to a laird in a grand lodge overlooking Badcall Bay near Scourie in Sutherland.

One afternoon in early May she saw her master drive away in his car and shortly afterwards felt inextricably depressed and sensed an overpoweringly dark feeling of bleak oppression which she vainly tried to shake off by diligently going about her household duties.

Then, while cooking lunch, she was startled to hear heavy footfalls in the hallway because she was certain there was nobody else on the premises.

Feeling distinctly uneasy, she hurried into the hall but there was no one there. Then she heard the steady, almost rhythmic tread of footsteps ascending the upper half of the staircase but this time there seemed to be two pairs of feet involved.

Her master's bedroom door seemed to close and there was the distinct sound of movement in this room which was just above her.

She went upstairs to investigate and knocked with some trepidation on her master's closed bedroom door. There was no reply and, on looking into the room, she found it was totally empty and just as the laird had left it, though there did seem to be the strange indentation of an invisible prone figure on the coverlet of the bed.

Believing she was imagining things, she returned to the kitchen and an hour later a car drove up the driveway. When she answered the knock on the front door, the housekeeper was greeted by the local police constable who informed her solemnly that he had received a phone call that the laird had been drowned in a small loch while attempting to save a lamb that had fallen into the water.

The constable said he was now en route to the scene of the accident and departed in his car, leaving the distraught housekeeper leaning shocked in the doorway.

Soon afterwards, the laird's car drove up the driveway with two estate workers bearing the dead man who was then carried up to his room and laid out on his bed.

The housekeeper noticed that the heavy boots of the estate workers ascending the stairs and placing their master on his bed sounded exactly the same as those she had previously heard a few hours ago at the precise moment when the laird had drowned.

Corrie of the Goblins

BEAUTIFUL, PLACID LOCH KATRINE takes its name from a lovely maiden who used to roam high up on adjacent Ben Venue. Where the picturesque loch now lies, so beloved of Sir Walter Scott, Queen Victoria and numerous subsequent tourists, there used to be a dry, fertile glen dotted with sheep and copses of trees where farmers lived an idyllic, pastoral life.

Up on the mountain was a waterfall where pure, crystal waters tumbled down into a river that wended through the farmlands far below. This water originated in an artificial dam constructed by villagers to channel precious irrigating moisture to their crops; and among the guardians appointed to keep watch over this important site was a farmer's daughter called Katrine.

However, in a nearby cave dwelt a malicious demon with red eyes and scaly skin, one of the dreaded uruisg or water imps who haunted and bedevilled lonely places.

From afar this horrid creature fell in love with the fair Katrine as she sat on rocks and sang songs to while away the time: but whenever he advanced on her, she spurned him and fled away.

As often happens in such cases, his burning love turned to bitter hate and one moonlit evening, as Katrine carefully watched over the dam, a handsome young Highlander in kilt and plaid strolled through the rustling heather towards her, offering her a share of his bowl of wild mountain berries.

Shyly, Katrine accepted, little knowing that this was in fact the demon in disguise and that the berries were drugged.

As she slumped into a deep slumber, the demon cut the sluices of the dam and down flowed and crashed thousands of gallons of pure water into the glen, drowning the villagers as they slept in their beds.

When Katrine eventually woke up in the bright moonlight and realised what had happened on her watch, she flung herself, grief stricken, into the seething waters and drowned.

The demon lived on and the wild screeches heard at night on the mountain are not eagles or foxes but the evil one yelling with glee at his wicked work.

Ben Venue is the traditional meeting place of the uruisgs and they regularly have black sabbaths on this lonely spot, earning it the local title of Corrie of the Goblins.

Scott mentioned these water demons several times in his epic poem *The Lady of the Lake* set on and around Loch Katrine.

For instance there are the lines -
> *A sharp and shrieking echo gave,*
> *Coir Uriskin, thy goblin cave!*

And also -
> *By many a bard in Celtic tongue,*
> *Has Coir Uriskin been sung.*
> *A softer name the Saxons gave*
> *And called the grotto Goblin Cave.*

The White Horseman

THE STORY of the ominous phantom horseman of north Sutherland began as far back as the battle of Bannockburn in the summer of 1314.

During the ferocious fighting with the English near the ramparts of Stirling Castle, one standard bearer after another carrying the personal banner of Robert the Bruce was brutally cut down, so that at one stage the flag lay trampled in the mud under thundering horses' hooves: but one warrior, Donald Gordon, snatched it up and galloped with it into the fray and hence to eventual victory.

The Bruce had witnessed Donald's reckless courage and in the aftermath of the conflict sent for him but he could not be found and somebody said they had seen him fall, mortally wounded.

In memory of his courage, Bruce then sent a silver brooch north to Kyle where Donald's brother Angus lived.

When the brooch finally arrived by special messenger, Angus boasted to all his neighbours that the talisman had been specially given to him in recognition of his martial valour. In fact, Angus had been heading south with a small force to take part in the battle but had been too late for the actual hostilities.

However, it turned out that Donald was not dead after all. He had indeed been seriously wounded, as might have been expected considering his bravery: but he had been taken in by a farmer's wife who proceeded to nurse him back to health and after a couple of months he was able to make the long trek home.

When he arrived back in his native village and heard about his brother's lies he was naturally furious and flung him out of the family home.

Angus sheltered in some nearby woods, surviving as best he could from berries plucked from bushes, too proud to ask for help.

There was a torrential downpour one night and Angus fell ill with pneumonia. He did manage to stagger home, begged his brother's forgiveness, which was grudgingly granted, but died a few days later in bed.

Donald felt guilty about turning his brother out and thereafter resolved to look after anyone in need as best he could and gradually gained a reputation as a Good Samaritan to all and sundry who crossed his path.

Astride his white horse, he was a regular sight on the northern roads, dispensing charity and giving aid when necessary.

While out fishing one day, he fell into the icy waters of a loch and floundered about freezing for hours until he was picked up and taken home: but, just like his brother, he was dead from pneumonia after just a few days in his bed.

Tragically his soul never found peace and his pale figure on horseback was regularly seen, though its presence became dreaded since its manifestation was often an omen of something bad about to happen, usually a death in the family.

The Amorous Monk

MELVILLE GRANGE FARM once stood in a stretch of open countryside deep in Midlothian, in the area between Edinburgh and Dalkeith, being part of the Melville Castle estate.

The farm stood on a site once a part of land owned by the diligent, holy monks of nearby Newbattle Abbey.

In the 14th century one of these monks, a novice, fell in love with a young woman whose father was a local landowner and the pair used to meet secretly for amorous trysts in the cottage at Melville Grange.

However, the girl's father found out and sternly forbade such a situation, insisting that the illicit liaison be terminated. Reluctantly, the girl bowed to paternal authority and agreed.

However, she still felt she had to explain the situation fully to her cowled admirer and set off to meet him. Her father decided to follow her and witnessed her going into the farm where she embraced the impatiently waiting monk who did not realise this was in fact a farewell gesture.

Flying into a furious rage, the watching farmer set the building alight and jammed the door, so that the screaming, hammering lovers were trapped inside and engulfed by the flames.

The cottage was burnt to the ground and then later rebuilt as a farmhouse and many witnesses over the centuries have claimed that they have seen the ghost of the hapless girl, clothed in a long, grey, medieval gown, stalking through the grassy grounds.

There have been no sightings of the monk, possibly because he was more pious and was therefore able to pass on to the other side, even though his sin was probably the greater. Still, maybe he did not go to Heaven.

The Devil Woman

THE GAELIC TERM luideag means the rag and was the derogatory term used to describe a vicious demon who haunted the bleak, moorland stretches round a small loch in eastern Skye.

She was described as being spindly, hideous in appearance with red rimmed, staring eyes and tattered garb, bony flesh, pointed claws and sharp fangs which she would hissingly bare if encountered.

She was thus definitely a creature to be avoided and if any man crossed her path, especially at night. he was liable to end up in the cold waters of the loch for, despite a skeletal thinness, she was nevertheless very strong and six foot in height.

According to tradition, she had been imprisoned by members of a rival clan in the deep dungeons of their keep during medieval times but had somehow managed to escape by twisting out of a drain and had then taken to her heels: but, in trying to shake off her pursuers by swimming across the loch, she had drowned in its black, peat-sodden depths.

Ever since she had haunted the lochside and sought revenge on any nocturnal male travellers who had the misfortune to wander past at the wrong time.

She particularly preyed on lost strangers but did not seem to have any interest in female victims.

She was last seen in the late 19th century wandering beside the road between Broadford and Sleat but had vanished completely after the chieftain of a local clan, a laird, had been found dead near the small loch.

At the time it was believed he had been killed by a wild animal of some kind for he had claw-like marks on his chest and neck and seemed to have been bitten repeatedly.

An expression of abject terror was on his face, frozen in death like a stone statue, and he had probably been fleeing, panic stricken, before slipping in the muddy bracken.

Locals speculated long afterwards just what particular savage creature could have singled him out and the fact that the spectral hag's hunting mission seemed to be over with the termination of the dead man's clan line indicated to the superstitious a more supernatural explanation.

The Wounded Deer

WILD AND DESOLATE, Rannoch Moor in the central Highlands was once the favourite hunting ground of a local clan chieftain called Donald Cameron.

While out one day trying to track down some red deer which he intended taking down with his trusty bow and arrows, he shot at a hind (a female deer) and wounded it in the shoulder: but, though he followed this crippled prey for several miles, catching glimpses of it staggering amongst the rocks and bracken, while tracing a trail of blood along the marshy ground, the deer managed to escape as darkness fell.

Months later, Donald was traversing the lonely, windswept moor when he was overtaken by a great tiredness and, seeing the shadows lengthen, decided to spend the night tucked under a huge, overhanging boulder.

He settled down, constructing for himself a makeshift heather-clad shelter made of branches and soon fell fast asleep, wrapped in his voluminous plaid.

However, his slumbers were visited by the vision of a beautiful woman who approached in a dream and offered him one of his own arrows, sighing plaintively, "Never did I believe you would ever harm me, Donald, after the many hours we have wandered together over the moor."

"But I have never seen you before or harmed you," protested Donald in the dream. "And where did you get my arrow?"

"I am the spirit of the hind you shot at," she answered reproachfully. "I am the fairest of my herd and many a happy day on the moor I have led you to, even though I am under enchantment."

The young man did not know what to do but accepted the strange gift of the arrow which he noticed was bloodstained at the tip. He solemnly promised in future only to shoot at mature stags and never at hinds.

Then the woman slowly, wistfully moved off, singing sadly to herself as she rejoined a distant herd of grazing deer.

When the cold dawn broke, Donald slowly awoke and stiffly stretched his limbs, muttering to himself, "What a strange yet realistic dream."

Then his hand touched something on the ground and he saw it was one of his old arrows, black with congealed blood.

The Wonder Bell

SAINT MERCHARD was one of the earliest Christian missionaries in the north of Scotland which at that time was still the realm of the Picts.

He set about preaching throughout Strathglass in the Western Highlands and his attention was drawn to a white cow which he passed every day but which seemed to be gazing down at an old tree's roots all the time.

She never seemed to eat but always was plump enough and, puzzled, the saint decided to dig at the roots and there he found three glistening bells, as new and burnished as if they had just come from their maker's hands.

He gave one each to his two followers and kept one for himself and it was then revealed to him in a dream that they should each set out in their own separate ways and build a church wherever their bell automatically rang out without any human aid.

Merchard travelled southwards towards Glenmoriston and his bell finally rang of its own volition beside a stream where he duly built his church.

He became the glen's patron saint and the miraculous bell had pride of place at the front of his church, curing all those who touched it in faith until the ageing building began to crumble and fall into ruin.

The bell was then reverently moved out into the churchyard and placed on a flattened tombstone specially set aside for it. It still rang of itself whenever a funeral was approaching and a corpse was carried nearby.

On one occasion it was heard ringing urgently in the middle of the night and, alarmed by this, some local folk ventured out to see what was amiss.

They found a man lying on the ground a few yards from the church's front door, stabbed to death. He had been robbed and a search was immediately made for the killer who, thanks to the bell's timely warning, was soon caught trying to make his escape over a nearby hill, his clothes still damp with his victim's blood.

This bell vanished in mysterious circumstances, probably stolen during a spring night in 1870, though it never rang in alarm which made locals think it was possibly taken by someone or something sympathetic to it, maybe even the ghost of the saint who had long since died and been put to rest in the same churchyard.

The Cursed Mansion

WINDHOUSE on the Shetland island of Yell is a country mansion now abandoned to the wild elements, in keeping with a curse placed on the premises by an old woman who was evicted from her croft at the start of the 19th century to make way for an expansion of the estate.

She declared to the ruthless laird who was flinging her out of hearth and home, "Neither you nor your family will prosper; and one day the sheep will wander through the middle of your home!"

This came true but her ghost also haunts the ruins, along with a sinister black dog and a young child regularly spotted in what used to be the kitchen.

There was also a fourth spectre, a heavily built man who walks through what is left of the gale-lashed, stone walls. He wears a dark cloak and hat and is a pedlar who was murdered in the grounds during a drunken argument.

In the midst of rebuilding work which embellished Windhouse in 1880, the skeleton of a man was found buried in the building's foundations and it was believed to be that of the pedlar.

The Windhouse lairds, who were a law unto themselves on the island, all had bad reputations; and one in particular was notorious for his cavalier attitude to the legal niceties, particularly when it came to land and property, hence his unfeeling eviction of the old woman.

He also tried to assault the local minister who remonstrated with him and the furious aristocrat had to be restrained by servants. He was also implicated in various other violent incidents, including the strange disappearance of the pedlar.

There were even rumours that a tax collector from the mainland, supposedly drowned at sea, had in fact been done away with on Yell; and also reports of a labourer, whose work was deemed unsatisfactory, being beaten to death, his body ending up buried under the kitchen windows in a patch of the garden where no flowers bloomed. The ghost child may also have something to do with the laird's homicidal temper.

The house, now incorporated into a bird sanctuary and thus left alone, was abandoned in 1930 but even these days the ruins still have a brooding, intimidating atmosphere and locals make sure they are nowhere nearby when darkness falls.

The Hag On the Moors

GLEN URQUHART in Inverness-shire was the setting for many a cattle rustling exploit and clan feud. It is scenic and peaceful now but its boulders and glades once rang with bloodcurdling screams which still echo down the centuries on dark, moonless nights.

There is hardly a sizeable rock or deep hollow that is not known by some local name, such as the Glade of Dead Men or the Stone of the Slaying or the Red Burn or some such lurid title.

The haunted woods were frequently visited by those with the Second Sight or psychic knowledge wishing to know what lay in store for them and they frequently witnessed vast shadowy hordes battling in the grey, misty skies over the moors, portents of fighting to come or memories of battles past.

Between Corrimony and Invermoriston lies a bleak stretch of wild country once haunted by the Hag of Chrathaich who had been jilted by a local MacMillan chieftain at the altar and who, totally distraught, had flung herself into the dark depths of Loch Meikle.

She used to accost solitary male wayfarers to find out their names and if it happened to be MacMillan she would engage his attention in a seductive manner, being able to change her appearance into a demure girl if she chose instead of her normal form as a wrinkled, old, grey corpse, still active like a Gaelic zombie.

While the unsuspecting MacMillan was distracted, she would steal his bonnet and then run off and, no matter how fast or lithely the MacMillan pursued her fleeing form, she would eventually disappear into the desolate moorlands with only a light wind remaining in his ears like her lamenting voice.

Once distant and alone, she would resume her hag-like form, sit down and rub the bonnet between two stones and, as the cloth wore thin, the MacMillan, who by this time was making his way breathlessly back home, began to feel lethargic and increasingly fatigued. When the hag on the moor managed to rub a hole big enough in his bonnet, he would drop down dead.

Finally the man she thought was going to be her husband, Donald MacMillan of Balmacaan who was now an old man, encountered her on the road, though, disguised as she was as a young girl, he did not recognise her. This time she did not run off for, as she grabbed at his bonnet, he managed to snatch it back and a fierce tussle ensued with his strength succeeding and he pulled the bonnet off her.

She then retreated to the moor but he did not follow and, silhouetted on the skyline, her human form became transfigured into that of a semi-transparent, skeletal, drowned old hag whose bony finger pointed down to him as she screamed, "You will die at nine of the clock, three nights hence!"

Then she disappeared over the hill.

Sure enough, at the fateful moment with his family gathered around him in the great hall of his castle, the MacMillan collapsed into his chair, clutching his chest – dead and ghastly white. For days his clansmen scoured the moor looking for the Hag to wreak their revenge but she was never seen again, though some of the searchers claimed they heard the sound of distant female laughter during their search.

Staked at the Crossroads

WITH A CIRCUITOUS OUTLET to the open sea, Loch Duich lies in the wilds of Wester Ross where Eilean Donan Castle, ancestral home of the MacRaes, stands strategically on a rocky islet at its entrance.

In its dark waters when his crop failed during harvest-time in the mid-19th century, a destitute farmer drowned himself and, once his corpse had been washed ashore and because he had been a devout member of his local kirk, it was buried in the little churchyard at Kintail on a hillock overlooking the loch.

However, as traditionally happened with a suicide, he was interred with his head not his feet pointing to the east so he would be unaware of the general Resurrection of the Blessed when it came.

But apparently this was not deemed enough of a mortal punishment since, shortly afterwards, the herring deserted Loch Duich in shoals.

Local fishermen, believing it might be a freak of nature, held out for a few months, hoping the fish would soon return but they did not do so.

A local seer who had the second sight told them that seven years was usually the length of time fish were absent after a murder or suicide in the immediate area, so the superstitious fishermen decided to do something about the situation.

One dark night they dug up the suicide's body and transported it, still in its coffin, to the top of a lonely hill where a winding pathway that led from Inverness-shire into Ross-shire bisected another roadway. A crossroads sign marked these boundaries.

There, as tradition demanded, they unscrewed the coffin lid and hammered a stake through the heart of the corpse.

They then reburied it at the crossroads where it was believed suicides' souls would be confused in their unmarked last resting places and not know which way to go, what with arrows above pointing in four directions over their graves.

Sure enough, this seemed to appease the nature gods and the herring returned in abundance to the loch that season and thereafter.

Dirges Over the Waters

NEAR FORT WILLIAM on the west Highland mainland, the road branches up to Corpach – or The Place of Bodies in Gaelic – at the head of Loch Linnhe, so named because during the Dark Ages and even throughout medieval times this used to be the spot from where marine, royal corteges embarked down the Firth of Lorn for final burials on the holy island of Iona way out to the western horizon.

If, as regularly happened, the waters were not calm enough for the black, funereal barges to sail, the whole mourning party would remain at Corpach until it was safe to set out.

Such funerals were conducted with much state and pomp since the deceased were usually kings or at least chieftains.

The final interment on Iona, which faced the setting sun and thus beyond it the mystical realm of Tir-nan-Og, an enchanted land where dwelt the souls of the blessed, involved ceremonies lasting up to eight days supervised by the Abbot and all his monks on the island, the body being laid out in state with full honours until the final hours.

The Lords of the Isles and the early Scottish Kings were all laid to rest in this holy ground where they were under the celestial protection of St Columba who had landed there to begin his sacred missionary work in what was then Caledonia.

Local fishermen and mariners have repeatedly related over the centuries and even into modern times that under certain climatic conditions, usually a calm, misty sea with darkening shadows round the Torran Rocks near Iona and just off the Mull coastline, the flickering lights from blazing torches on a long funeral fleet have been seen glimmering through the mirk on the black waters; and sometimes, though unseen, a mournful dirge from dozens of monks has been heard echoing from these spectral barges, dismal chants that have sent shivers down the spines of any who have had the misfortune to detect them.

The Black Hand

ON THE SPRAWLING Abergeldie estate, six miles from Ballater in the hilly hinterlands of Aberdeenshire, stood the ancient Mill of Inver beside the Fearder Burn where it entered the River Dee: and this building had been occupied for generations by a family called Davidson.

The area had also been haunted by a strange manifestation locally known simply as the Black Hand until one wintry night in 1767 when the current proprietor of the mill, one John Davidson, decided to investigate the phenomenon.

Stationing himself in the shadow of the mill, John waited patiently for more than an hour in the freezing darkness; then, on glancing upwards, he, like many others before him, was startled to see a bony, hairy hand floating on its own in mid-air, seemingly cut off bloodily at the wrist and unattached to any form, spectral or otherwise, a terrifying sight which had petrified locals for decades.

However, John was made of sterner stuff – this was his property after all – and he immediately and bravely challenged the hand, demanding to know what it wanted.

He then felt himself being overcome by what seemed a huge, suffocating presence and a sepulchral voice related how the hand had been severed in a duel and would not rest until the weapon which had done the deed was unearthed from wherever it lay, bloodstained and buried.

The hand then floated along and stopped abruptly, pointing urgently at the ground.

At dawn the next morning John was out on that same spot, digging deeply with his spade in the corner of the yard indicated by the hand and he eventually shoveled up a basket-hilted broadsword with a rusty blade which he proceeded to hang up like a trophy over his fireplace.

There were no reports of the Black Hand ever being seen again after that and neighbours were not slow to congratulate John on his courage.

Home of the Ghouls

THERE IS A WILD, UPLAND MOOR near Cromarty, five miles east of Invergordon, which once had a reputation as being a window into the afterlife.

On certain stormy nights, ghoulish phantoms were seen flying in and out of the swaying, surrounding trees like bats, while ghostly knights in armour still repeatedly clashed in battle, wrinkled old hags cackled demoniacally and lovely, fair haired maidens lured gullible male wayfarers deep into dark, viscous swamps from which there was no escape.

One stormy night a local fisherman happened to be crossing the moor when suddenly the air became chillier and darker and he saw in front of him, not grey, moonlit tufts of barren bracken, but a heaving, wave-tossed stretch of water, foam flecked and sparkling as far as he could glimpse into the distant gloom.

He could distinctly hear thundering waves and stood transfixed as a fishing boat ploughed slowly into view through the gale. To his astonishment he recognised the four occupants – three local fishermen plus his own brother.

Suddenly a huge wave seemed to engulf the frail looking craft and covered it, at which point the viewing fisherman fainted on the spot and sank to the ground.

Coming to after a few minutes, he rubbed his eyes and looked around but could see nothing but the rain-lashed moor. There was no sign of any seascape or creamy waves in the moonlight between scudding grey clouds.

Believing it all to have been some kind of hallucination, he told nobody about it for fear of derision: but the following morning there was a sudden squall off the coast which hit his village's fishing fleet.

Among the drowned washed up on the shore were the four men he had seen in his dream.

To his dying day, the heartbroken fisherman deeply regretted keeping the gloomy vision to himself and failing to warn the men of what might be in store for them out at sea.

A Devil For the Women

BALNAGOWAN HOUSE, four miles south of Tain in Ross and Cromarty and the former seat of the local Clan Ross who gave their name to the county, is haunted by Black Andrew Munro whose heavy, ponderous footsteps can be heard solemnly walking along the building's Red Corridor near where he met his violent death.

Andrew was the brutal, sadistic laird who ruled this particular roost in the middle of the 16th century before the Clan Ross took over his fortified bastion for themselves.

Among Andrew's many sordid depredations was forcing female farm workers to labour naked in the harvest fields regardless of the weather and he was also the perpetrator of rapes and murders for miles around.

Eventually and not before time, the chief of the Clan Ross, the feudal lord of this Highland district, tired of Andrew's reckless ways and the villain was unceremoniously flung out of a high window in his own home by muscular Ross clansmen, a rope round his neck so that he was suitably hanging out of one of the bedrooms where he used to have his way with servant girls.

Notorious as 'a devil for the women', Andrew's evil, leering face can still be seen in the shadows of the corridor, a sight described by one witness as "a hairy, old man with burning, malevolent, bloodshot eyes glowering in the gloom" whenever a new female guest arrives at the house.

On such occasions no dog with its hackles up will even enter the Red Corridor but sinister steps can be heard walking up and down, restlessly on the prowl for fresh female flesh as in days of yore.

The Galloping Lover

AN ANCIENT ROADWAY in Midlothian, once an important route linking Dalkeith and Peebles but now little used, has become an overgrown moorland track haunted by a galloping, wild eyed horseman.

The roots of this phantom lie in the late 19th century when a strapping, young labourer, who worked on one of the local farms, used to regularly borrow his master's horse so that he could ride the seven miles to Eddleston village where he was courting a local beauty.

Each midnight after his amatory tryst he would ride back to the farm and return the trusty steed to its stable before the animal was missed.

One moonlit night as he was galloping pell-mell across the moor, the labourer heard the sound of a man groaning in agony and spotted an upturned cart which had been bearing a load of limestone from a nearby quarry which was now spread all over the road. The horse pulling the cart had broken loose and bolted.

Not wanting to miss his rendezvous with his lover or indeed be caught with the borrowed horse which he had never gained permission to use, the labourer turned his face away coldly and rode past the prone figure under the cart pleading for help.

On his return trip towards dawn, the labourer likewise sped past the upturned cart but noticed the injured man was now lying silent and immovable.

In fact, the dying carter was not found until later in the day when a search party came across him.

The fatally injured man, before passing away, managed to muster enough strength to relate with his last breath how the labourer, who he had recognised, had ignored him twice and had simply galloped past unheeding.

Word soon spread and nobody would even talk to the labourer who was held responsible for the carter's untimely death.

The wretched outcast was sacked from his job, his lover deserted him and within days he had vanished.

His bloodstained corpse was later found sprawled on a deserted stretch of moorland, his throat cut and it was assumed he had committed suicide: but there was also another grim theory that relatives of the fatally injured carter had murdered him in revenge for his deliberate callousness.

Whatever the cause of death, the ghost of the labourer and his phantom, ill-gotten steed can still be seen of a starry night on the lonely path over the wilderness between Cauldhall and Cockmuir, racing to his urgent tryst again and again.

High Spirited Spectres

GHOSTS NORMALLY HAVE a sinister reputation for making gloomy, foreboding appearances but this was not the case at Monymusk House in mid-Aberdeenshire where the phantoms were apparently out for a good time, even in the afterlife.

There were several such apparitions at the old pile beside Monymusk village which is really more of an ancient castle than a house, despite its name, towering over the peacefully meandering River Don.

One playful ghost was the Grey Lady who mostly manifested from a cupboard in the nursery from where she happily and harmlessly joined in games with any children who usually in their gleeful innocence were strangely unafraid and sometimes even exhilarated by her supernatural presence.

Then there was the so-called Party Ghost who usually made uninvited appearances at social functions, pushing his way to the bar when a large group was celebrating, joining in the general carousing. He was always immaculately dressed in a kilt and made a striking, distinctive presence.

The third ghost has been regularly spotted sitting in the library, even into the present day, and chortling over a private joke as he peruses a book and who vanishes instantly into thin air when challenged.

The fourth ghosts, a male and female, have never actually been seen but have been distinctly heard behind closed doors in one of the bedrooms, the lascivious groans of their delight ending with giggles of pleasure at hidden sensations.

Their rising squeals can clearly be heard but, when the door is flung open wide, nobody is there and silence rules, the sheets being undisturbed on an immaculately made bed.

Another phantom phenomenon involves ghostly footsteps that regularly run up and down the stairs but why they are doing so has remained a mystery, though it has been remarked that they seem to be the light-footed steps of a woman eagerly rushing to an upstairs bedroom which would certainly fit in with the merry ghosts of this particular abode.

The Fatal Ford

A SHALLOW STRETCH of the scenic River Connon, near Brahan Castle which was built in the 17th century by the local feudal lord, the Earl of Seaforth, was long reputed to be haunted by a malignant water wraith who used to arrange fatal accidents for the unwary on moonless nights.

No explanation was forthcoming for its murderous malice, though there was a legend that it was the ghost of a vengeful, married lady's lover who was drowned – or more precisely bound by the bodyguards of the angry husband who passed judgement and executed the lover by tossing him in the river – who in turn was determined to wreak vengeance on innocent passers-by, forcing them to share his watery fate.

One of the most detailed accounts of this marine manifestation concerned a manservant of the Seaforths who, late one night after a celebration, was accompanied by two drunken cronies wending their way home, the wayward group either forgetting or not caring or defiant about the ford's evil reputation.

The servant, a young, vigorous fellow mounted on a powerful horse, prompted his steed into the dark, swirling but shallow water and tried to ride across but half way over he emitted a loud scream of terror and there was a frightful snorting, stamping, whinnying and splashing as the horse's prancing hooves seemed to fight the river.

The servant's two wide-eyed companions were then horrified to see a tall, shadowy, shapeless form arise, roaring in fury from the depths, looming blackly over their friend, seizing him by the throat and dragging him down into the swirling currents.

A moment later, its rider unhorsed, the struggling steed waded towards the opposite bank which it managed to scramble up.

The servant fought valiantly against his demonic adversary before vanishing forever beneath the creamy waves as his companions took to their heels into the darkness.

The Fairies' Farewell

ONE SPRING SUNDAY MORNING in the early 18th century, a little herd boy and his sister were privileged to witness the fairies forever leaving the Black Isle, that picturesque peninsula (not really a complete island) stretching out between the Cromarty and Moray Firths.

The children dwelt in a clachan (a small Highland village) called Burn of Eathie on the south side of the steep sided glen down which a small stream tumbled in a series of falls, at the bottom reaching a scenic, rocky bay a mile from Cromarty.

That morning everyone in the huddle of cottages had attended the local kirk, for it was a God fearing community like most rural hamlets at the time, so the two children, too young for church, were left to their own devices and were playing out in the open air when up the sunny glen they heard the approach of a cavalcade of tiny figures on their small mounts. The latter were shaggy, diminutive creatures, speckled dun and grey, while their riders were ugly dwarves with nothing of the spectral beauty depicted in glowingly beautiful fairy paintings.

They were dressed in dusty medieval jerkins with faded tartans, plain cloaks and little red caps from under which their uncombed hair shot out over their craggy features.

The two children stood gazing in astonishment at this little parade as the uncouth cavalcade trooped past into the brown bracken that covered the hills.

The boy finally felt compelled to ask the last rider before they all disappeared, "Who are ye, little mannie? And where're ye goin'?"

To which the creature scowled faintly, "Never of the race of Adam. We are the people of peace who shall nevermore be seen in Scotland."

They seemed like the last remnants of a lost, defeated race, a retreating army, dejected as they trooped away.

The children never forgot this revelation and related it to their parents when the latter came back from church; and the story was then handed down through the generations.

There was no explanation as to why the wee fairy folk were departing so disconsolately and no record of what happened to them. The impending inroads of industrialisation may have had something to do with their exodus but such a parade was never again seen in the land.

Black Duncan of the Castles

EDINAMPLE CASTLE is a z-shaped ruin with several old, crumbling towers which stands on the southern shores of Loch Earn in Perthshire.

It was one of seven such stone fortresses obsessively built by the proud and arrogant Sir Duncan Campbell of Glenorchy who lived from 1553 until 1631 and ruled his fiefdom in central Scotland like royalty, dispensing his own form of rough justice and doing as he wanted with his subdued tenants.

He was keen on constructing so many bastions and keeps because he was determined his extensive estates would be secure and under a feudal iron fist, thus controlling his 'serfs' and earning him the nickname Black Duncan of the Castles.

Edinample caused more than its fair share of building problems, however, not least because the labourers involved proved lazy, unenthusiastic and inefficient.

The moody, quixotic laird had insisted that various personal quirks be incorporated into the designs and architecture to suit his particular tastes; and, on what was supposed to be the completion date of the castle's construction, Black Duncan, who had been away during the latter months of building, went into one of his notorious fits of anger when he noticed that the builders had somehow forgotten to construct a parapet walk around the roof of one of the towers overlooking the lochside.

When told he was not getting a penny for his incompetent work, the chief mason foolishly insisted on showing the laird how he could still take a walk round the top of the tower: but, as he scrambled about the slates high above the ground and beside the mason, watched by a small crowd of workers far below, the disappointed laird's anger mounted as he became convinced they were all making a fool of him.

Suddenly pulling a pistol from his belt, the laird shot the chief mason through the heart and the dying man toppled from the roof, plummeting down to the ground far below with an ear piercing scream.

Ever since, the sad spirit of the mason has regularly been seen making his lonely, despairing walk amidst the old castle's ruins in the twilight, apparently still doggedly determined to prove it was possible to circumnavigate the roof, a wasted vigil since the proposed parapet was never built, Black Duncan having gone off the idea.

Skeletons in the Dark

DARKLY OMINOUS and threatening as it once was, Cromarty Castle no longer exists but strange stories connected with it have come down through the centuries, some retained within the dusty annals of the parish.

Originally built as a grim keep in the early 13th century, this forbidding castle was eventually demolished in the second half of the 18th century to make way for a more comfortable, fashionable and stylish Georgian country house completed in the 1770s.

The old castle of ill repute used to stand beside the small, thriving fishing community of Cromarty on a promontory projecting into the Firth of the same name on Scotland's furthest north eastern coastline; and, during the long winter nights of its occupation, residents used to hear weird noises within the soaring, stone walls which varied from loud groans to agonised screams and the ethereal sound of phantom footsteps shuffling along the dark, draughty corridors.

Most of the awful sounds of human anguish came from deep within the bowels of the castle, well below ground level.

Grey figures vanishing into solid walls were also reported and some of these phantoms were said to be headless.

Much of this was simply put down to overwrought imaginations until the time came when the old castle was being partly demolished and renovated and workmen found that one of the walls in the deepest dungeon had an unearthly echo and obviously contained a secret chamber of some sort.

On knocking down some masonry, they found to their terrified amazement, as they held up flickering lamps in the icy darkness, that lying on the bare, stone floor of the empty, extensive hollow uncovered lay a large white pile of crumbling human bones, stark in the dancing shadows.

When the cluttered skeletons were gradually, meticulously and finally pieced together, it was found there were twenty, some missing their heads which were never found. How or why they had met their gruesome end was not for once officially recorded in the parish annals but those who had witnessed the restless, headless spirits and who knew nothing of the hidden chamber had seemingly been telling the truth.

The north east was once bloodily fought over by vicious

Mackenzie and Urquhart clansmen, so it is possible the entombed corpses were the result of this long feud which went on for centuries.

One local 18th century Sheriff described the area as "this vagrant and savagely incomprehensible county of Cromarty!"; so the locale certainly had a long, bloodstained, notorious reputation for brutal lawlessness and unrestrained violence.

A Dream House

BALLACHULISH HOUSE in Argyll was once owned by Sir Harold Boulton, composer of the 'Skye Boat Song', who testified to the various ghosts that haunted his home, including a fierce-looking Highlander who walked through walls, a trooper who galloped up and down the gravel driveway who eventually dismounted, knocked on the main door then vanished, as well as a tinker who was in the habit of frequenting the main gate on autumn evenings.

The place should have been haunted anyway because it was here that Captain Campbell was ordered to set in motion the infamous Massacre of Glencoe during which his rivals, the MacDonalds, were decimated in their beds just a few miles away.

Sir Harold also told a strange tale concerning his mother who, long before he moved to Scotland and while she was resident in central London, regularly spoke of "a beautiful rural house somewhere up north" which haunted her dreams so much that she could itemise its details, though she had no idea where exactly it was or what the connection was with the Boulton family.

Imagine her surprise when on a Highland tour with her son one summer, she came across Ballachulish House and recognised it as the place that obsessed her slumbers though she had never in reality visited it before.

She told as much to the house owner, Lady Beresford, and described a long, ornate staircase that used to be a central feature of the mansion but which had long since been bricked up and was now out of sight.

Lady Beresford then scrutinised Mrs Boulton with uncharacteristic bad manners, pointed at the visitor and declared that it was indeed she or at least her astral body which, though obviously not dead, had regularly and at night silently been haunting the corridors and scaring her family for years.

They had assumed it was the spectre of a former occupant and not an image of someone still very much alive and well down in London.

A few months after this meeting, Lady Beresford died peacefully in her bed and the Boultons felt somehow strangely obliged to buy the house where they went on to spend many happy years, as if at long last they had come home.

Starving Spectres

SCOTTISH GHOSTS are often the apparitions of people who met violent, often tortured deaths and that was certainly the case concerning ghosts who haunt the stone corridors of Hermitage and Dalhousie Castles.

The latter is a formidable medieval keep dominating the South River Esk near Bonnyrigg in Midlothian once owned by the Ramsay clan who gained their prestigious position after fighting valiantly for Scottish independence from the rebellious days of William Wallace onwards.

The family were made Earls of Dalhousie but carried on their belligerent ways through various clan feuds with equally aggressive, acquisitive neighbours.

One set of powerful rivals was the Douglas faction in Lanarkshire and in 1342 after a brutal skirmish Sir Alexander Ramsay was captured by the forces of Sir William Douglas who took their aristocratic captive to the forbidding dungeons of Hermitage Castle in the Borders.

There Ramsay was chained to a wall and starved to death, his ordeal being prolonged for three weeks because grains of corn would trickle down into his cell through a hole from the granary which happened to be situated directly above the dungeon.

Ever after, his restless, groaning spirit has haunted the ruins.

Likewise, Dalhousie Castle has its own ghost, a grey lady who has been seen regularly in one of the buildings' old turrets and on one of the winding staircases leading to it.

Her rustling gown has also been heard and she is believed to have been a Lady Catherine whose details were never officially recorded but according to oral tradition was the mistress of one of the lairds.

His wife found out about the relationship and lured Lady Catherine into the castle on some pretext; then enticed her into a turret room, turned the key and starved her to death, despite her muffled screams and pleas which decreased as the days passed, the laird being away at the time. What thoughts of sweet revenge went through his wife's mind over these crucial days and nights can only be imagined.

Thereafter, Lady Catherine's restless spirit has haunted the castle.

The laird's wife took great pleasure in telling her husband on his return about the corpse in the tower. He was heartbroken and gave his lover a decent burial in the local kirkyard: but there was nothing he could do about her ghost which eventually drove him mad with tormented manifestations, so that he ended up flinging himself from the tower where she had starved to death.

His distraught wife had to vacate the premises and live elsewhere because of the spectre which haunted the castle but whether her dead husband joined his mistress in phantom appearances is not recorded, though it is likely.

Down in the Vaults

THE NATIONAL LIBRARY OF SCOTLAND in Edinburgh has at least one ghost whose presence has been well attested over the years. Down in a storage basement area, known by staff simply as 'the vaults', the manifestation of a Highland chieftain in full regalia has been regularly seen.

A typical sighting was in 1973 when a female member of the staff was sent down to the area to file away some papers and books.

The musty, dusty, shadowy shelves had a reputation for being darkly eerie but the woman had no information about any spectres. While working away with the files, she suddenly felt the temperature plunge coldly.

On turning round to seek the source of the chilliness in the air, she saw standing just a few feet away the towering figure of a clansman in his kilt, bonnet and plaid.

Quite distinctive, even in the half light, was the intricate silver brooch holding his plaid in place, a glistening ornament adorned by swirling Celtic artwork. The chieftain moved slightly then put out his hands to the librarian, gazing into her eyes.

Then she noticed his wrists were manacled together with dangling, stout, iron chains.

This phantom terrified her but she gathered her wits, muttered a short prayer and fled the scene.

She later discovered that the library had been built on the site of an old prison in which Highland rebels were regularly held, often before their execution on the public block.

There was no doubt in her mind that she had seen the ghost of a prisoner who had been allowed to starve to death in the prison dungeons, a fate regularly meted out to troublemakers in days gone by.

The Magic Herd

ONE AFTERNOON in the autumn of 1938, Mary Falconer, who lived at Achlyness in the western Highlands, was taking a shortcut with a female friend through the hills to Ardchullin with some fresh venison in a sack slung over her shoulder.

On nearing Loch Garget Beag, she noticed a number of wild ponies grazing by the water and, thinking that one of the animals – a white one – actually belonged to her neighbour who had reported it as missing, she decided to make use of it to carry her load along the winding track over the heather-clad braes.

However, on walking towards the pony she came within a few feet of it and saw that it was much bigger than the missing one and that there was a garland of water lilies and weeds round its neck.

The eyes of the animal and the woman met and she realised she was looking at an each uisge, kelpie or water horse which then proceeded to lead the other dozen ponies into the loch where they all swam out to the middle and then plunged to the depths.

The residents of nearby Kinlochbervie were convinced that the loch was home to a whole herd of these mystical creatures who were not entirely innocent because they regularly had the supernatural knack of taking the form of handsome young males who could seduce vulnerable women in the neighbourhood.

Lochs were often dragged and even drained to rid them of water horses and this happened once in the Sleat district of Skye where a large net was used and an entangled object the size of a horse was dragged up.

However, the searchers involved lost their nerve and ran off so they never found out if they had ensnared the legendary creature or not.

Miss Falconer and her companion were lucky to have escaped from their confrontation unscathed, possibly because they were both known as seers with occult powers. There was hardly a death in the area that they were not able to foretell which was more a curse than a blessing since they were able to visualise funerals in advance and the number of mourners and conveyances involved.

On one occasion they saw the long bracken flatten under the feet of invisible mourners coming from a certain house long before the funeral actually took place.

As for water horses, they have not been forgotten, for huge statues representing equine heads called The Kelpies are now a landmark near Falkirk.

The Dog At Dusk

IN LOCHABER during the late 19th century a long, winding path once snaked up over a lonely moor near some villages; and in 1897 travellers walking along this wild track started reporting the same type of weird incident. As dusk fell a large black dog would suddenly appear from nowhere and stare at them with green, baleful eyes that seemed both hypnotic and luminous.

Its paws did not seem to be touching the ground but somehow wayfarers were not unduly alarmed by any of this.

Each time the dog led them by some magnetic pull a hundred yards off the path where the docile animal then began to scrabble madly in the heather and dirt as if trying to retrieve a bone.

But it seemed to give up after a few minutes before staring at the traveller it had lured there and then simply vanished into invisibility.

The witnesses to this phenomenon were then startled awake as if from a dream and went on their way, baffled.

This happened regularly at the same spot and at the same time and it may have been expected that some kind of exploration of the ground would have taken place but this did not happen until a downpour of torrential rain one spring swept away some of the earth and exposed what appeared to be an old satchel.

Some of the nearby villagers then decided to dig on this spot so favoured by the phantom dog and soon they uncovered the decaying, bludgeoned corpse of an old pedlar who had vanished from the area years previously.

The authorities carried out a post mortem and it was found the body had indeed been killed due to head blows, presumably robbed and then hastily buried on the moor.

The corpse was interred in the nearest kirkyard and the black dog was never seen again. Locals recalled an old pedlar who used to frequent the area and who had a dog as a pet and travelling companion. What happened to it was never ascertained.

The Musical Cave

A LEGEND grew up in the 18th century concerning a local worthy in Arbroath on the north east Angus coastline called Tam Tyrie who, along with his wife and dog, supposedly went for a summer stroll along the beach until they came to caves three miles south of the town.

Tam was fond of playing the bagpipes and he was busy at this stridently musical pastime when a heavy shower of rain sweeping in from the North Sea onto the craggy coastline caused the three of them to shelter in a dark, echoing cave.

A witness later claimed that Tam's pipes could be clearly heard skirling away in the eerie, clammy, rocky blackness of the cave, probably to cheer the wayfarers up, until the sound vanished in the distance – and none of the trio were ever seen again, nor were their bodies ever recovered.

But on certain nights passers-by, too numerous to be mistaken, claimed they heard the echoing strains of Tam's bagpipes coming from the depths of the cave.

Cynics claimed this tall tale was merely a smart ploy on the part of local smugglers who used the caves to unload and store their illicit cargoes from vessels offshore on moonless nights, the idea being to use supposedly ghostly pipes to frighten off anyone snooping around.

Certainly this part of the coast was once notorious for smuggling, particularly when it came to French brandy and wine. Ships would lie beyond the horizon, only coming inshore after nightfall to avoid the attentions of the ever vigilant excisemen.

The only argument against the trick theory is that the phantom piping was reported long after the heady days of smuggling were over; and some smugglers themselves admitted that, although they landed barrels of illicit booze in sandy coves near Arbroath, they always avoided that particular cave which was said to be haunted.

The Bloody Stair

ROTHESAY CASTLE on the island of Bute in the Firth of Clyde was built in the late 12th century, a circular stone structure that was actually more a tower than a castle and which was surrounded by a deep moat.

However, it was not set in an area with particular defensive potential and as a medieval military bastion proved deficient.

So it was no real surprise when a dozen Norse longboats beached in the bay and marauding Vikings were able to besiege and eventually take the castle, despite the occupants resorting to the desperate act of pouring molten metal down on them from the high battlements.

The Vikings made a moveable tunnel out of felled trees to catch the metal. With upturned shields and working in relays the Norsemen hacked away at the wooden drawbridge until they made a sizeable hole.

Charging into the courtyard, the Vikings eventually put all the defenders to the sword, apart from a local aristocrat called Lady Isobel.

The invaders' leader declared that she would make a suitable partner for him and to show his ardour he chased her around various rooms until she managed to dash in terror to a stairway located between the outside circular perimeter wall and the gable of the chapel which gave access to the tower's first floor.

Running up the stairs, Isobel pulled a dagger from the belt of her long dress and screamed back at her pursuer that she would never give herself to him.

Then she plunged the knife repeatedly into her body and collapsed mortally wounded as scarlet stains spread down over the stone steps.

Ever after the spot was notorious as the Bloody Stair and her spectre was seen running upwards and screaming defiance.

The castle was again occupied by Vikings in 1263, this time by King Haakon of Norway en route to his decisive defeat at the battle of Largs, the resulting victory for the Scots meaning that no longer would longships prowl these waters looking for prey.

To make it more defensible, four additional towers were added in 1300 and an impressive gatehouse completed in 1541.

Restored in the 19th century by the third Marquis of Bute, the castle was placed in the guardianship of the state in 1951: but, regardless of any additions to the building, Isobel's ghost continued with her hauntings, terrifying anyone in the immediate vicinity.

The Housebound Wife

IN 1780 A LABOURER called George Gourlay and his growing family occupied a flat in a tall stone tenement in the steep close of Bell's Wynd off Edinburgh's High Street and he eventually decided he needed more living space than these cramped, crowded quarters.

To this end he approached his landlord's factor, pointing out that there was a larger, empty flat on the floor below his that he would like to move into: but for some inexplicable reason his landlord, Patrick Guthrie, was adamant that this would not be possible. Yet the flat remained unoccupied.

Puzzled by all of this on the part of his usually money conscious landlord, Gourlay decided to investigate on his own and easily burst into the flat via the old battered door hanging precariously on its hinges.

Wandering around in the claustrophobic gloom, he was baffled to find rooms still completely, even richly furnished, though a layer of dust lay over everything.

Suddenly there was a groaning sound behind him and Gourlay whirled round to confront the ghastly white phantom of a woman with staring, red eyes and grasping, bony arms stalking towards him in what looked like a diaphanous shroud.

Fear icily clutching his heart and terrified out of his wits, Gourlay not only fled out of the hanging door but also out of the building and did not stop until he had reached the city offices of the local Procurator Fiscal or law officer to whom he told his tale.

To Gourlay's astonishment he was then promptly charged with breaking and entering, possibly while of unsound mind, and the Fiscal took along two of his officials to investigate the empty flat where, after an extensive search, they plied up loose floorboards and found the mummified corpse of a grey, wrinkled, old woman preserved by the cold, dry conditions in her makeshift tomb.

Guthrie was then sought out and questioned and he admitted that years previously he had returned home early one evening and found his wife in bed with another man, as a result of which there was a violent quarrel during which blows were exchanged. The wife was so badly injured in the fracas that she died shortly afterwards from her injuries.

The lover, who had fled just after Guthrie's premature arrival, was a high ranking nobleman whose involvement would have caused a serious scandal for the authorities.

The Fiscal duly decided to quietly drop the case and the corpse was given a secret burial in the local kirkyard.

Nevertheless, she did not rest easy for her phantom form was still seen regularly stalking Bell's Wynd for years afterwards.

Meanwhile, Gourlay moved his family out to other premises with no explanation on his part.

The Bogle of Bogandoran

A BOGLE was an old Highland word for an apparition, a phantom that could somehow transform itself into a human-looking form. It could also mean a scarecrow, as in tattie-bogle.

Bogles took great delight in scaring the wits out of people and they were usually solitary creatures haunting desolate places where they would lie in hiding, ready to spring out on any unsuspecting traveller on the road during the hours of darkness.

One notorious bogle lurked near Bogandoran village on the outskirts of the Perthshire moors near a spot known locally as the Bog of Torrans and it used to carry an array of weapons with which it would give any victim a choice to use in a duel.

Unlucky wayfarers stopped by this bogle in their path had no option but to accept the challenge if they wanted to continue on their way and many a traveller deeply regretted setting out on the darkening open road when they ended up with sword or bullet wounds or a severe bruising.

The bogle never actually killed anyone but encounters with it left lifelong terrified impressions on the hapless victims who were then cursed with recurrent nightmares.

But on one occasion a doughty traveller, a local, muscular farmhand, managed to fight off the bogle by wielding a hefty cudgel.

Emboldened and encouraged by strong drink, the farmhand saw no reason why he should not pass the same spot again at the same hour but this simply enraged the bogle who then tried to push him over a steep precipice into a burn.

A bitter struggle then ensued which only ended with the bogle being stabbed through the heart by the farmhand's dirk. The creature toppled into the heather and the farmhand ran off to get some help but when the party of cautious locals returned with lamps from a nearby tavern they found only the impression of a deformed demonic, dwarf-like creature in the undergrowth but no trace of any body, alive or otherwise.

After that, travellers were able to walk the road at night without any fear of being attacked by a supernatural creature.

In the Borders, bogles were a kindlier breed who always had a soft spot for widows, orphans and other needy folk, often taking up their cause against persecutors.

The Robed Terror

THE NEW OWNERS of a large, rambling, old house at Ardnadam beside Dunoon on the Firth of Clyde moved in at the beginning of the 20th century.

One stormy evening they were terrified to see the grim-looking figure of a tall, bewhiskered man in a scarlet red turban and silk dressing gown slowly ascending the main stairs.

There was something forbidding about the phantom because of the way this transparent apparition in his voluminous robe climbed the steps as if he was going to his doom on the gallows and he always had a look of abject despair on his features.

Another strange contradiction was that, though he was dressed in Asiatic style, his face was distinctly Scottish, indeed a very pale white.

On another occasion the occupants heard the sound of something heavy being dragged across the floor of the attic but were too scared to investigate.

The new owners decided to research the history of the place they now inhabited, so they went to the files in the local library and also quizzed some of the older folk in the neighbourhood and gradually a story fell into place and the hauntings began to make some sense.

The old house had once belonged to a colonel who had served with a Scottish regiment in India, then part of the British Empire, who had adopted the dress of the sub-continent in his leisure hours, a habit he brought back with him when he returned to retire in his native Argyll.

On learning in his late seventies that he had a terminal tropical illness, he went up to his attic, dressed in turban and flowing gown, where he dragged a large piece of furniture across the trap door so that he would not be interrupted. He then read his Bible and after a while took out his old service revolver from the folds of his robe and, taking off his turban, shot himself in the head.

Once they had ascertained the facts of the case, the house owners realised the ghost meant them no harm so they left it in peace whenever they saw it which was very rarely and usually only on windy, rain-lashed nights.

This was one old soldier who not only did not die but did not even fade away.

The Dancing Vampires

FOUR STALKERS WERE OUT hunting deer in the spring of 1790 near Kinlochewe in the west Highlands when darkness fell quickly as it tends to do at that time of year and it proved too late to find their way back to their lodgings so, when they spotted in a wooded glen an empty, stone, hut-like shelter used by shepherds and herdsmen, they made their way there, lit a fire and settled down for the night.

They had caught some game earlier in the day and were able to cook a meal, cosily augmented by a small supply of whisky they had brought along in their supplies.

The post-repast, languorous mood was so mellow that one of the hunters started crooning a Gaelic love song which soon developed into some jaunty mouth music meant to emulate bagpipes playing a jig and his companions rose to their feet and started dancing, their shadows grotesque in the leaping firelight.

As they pranced around, one of them shouted, "Oh, if only we had some women to dance with!"

At that, as if in miraculous answer to the summons, the door burst open and four young women came skipping in. Three grabbed astonished partners while the fourth sat down with the music maker.

The men laughed in delight, asked no questions and danced

wildly as the music seemed to take on a life of its own, getting quicker, louder and carefree. It seemed like there were actually some invisible musicians in the room.

Suddenly one of the men noticed scarlet stains beginning to gather on the stony, straw-covered floor and noticed it was from a wound in the neck of one of his unaware companions too busy yelling in abandoned delight to feel he had been wounded.

Then as the wild women kicked their legs in the air, he saw that underneath their flashing white skirts were cloven hooves and furry ankles.

Horrified, he dashed for the door and out into the cold, dark night, pursued by his now sibilantly hissing partner.

He made it safely to a small, walled, circular enclosure containing horses and jumped in among them. For some reason this seemed to put his pursuer off the scent as she pulled up at the stone dyke, sniffing the air with flared nostrils.

Waiting until he thought the coast was clear, the stalker then jumped the dyke's wall and found his way through the darkness to the nearest village which he entered just as dawn broke.

A party of men led by the hunter then made their way back up the glen to the shieling.

On opening the door, which was already creaking ajar in the wind, they found the bodies of the three men on the floor, their corpses drained white, the blood sucked from their veins.

They had been the unwitting victims of a form of female vampire, the baobhan sith, demons who feasted on human blood. These creatures were adept at taking beautiful, seductive forms which men found hard to resist. They wore long, white dresses to conceal their devilish hooves and it was said they also had the ability to turn themselves into ravens or crows at will.

The Doonie of Crichope Linn

DOONIES were supernatural apparitions, usually old women, who suddenly manifested themselves in Scottish wildernesses to help people in trouble.

One typical incident involved a boy who started to climb a precipitous cliff face above a small, deep loch known as Crichope Linn near Thornhill in Dumfriesshire. He had spotted young rock doves high up on a ledge and wanted to catch one and take it home as a caged pet.

After excitedly clambering up a considerable height, he suddenly realised, to his frozen horror, that he was stuck and could neither ascend or descend.

Grabbing a nearby overhanging branch that looped out of a hazel bush in a crevice, he knew with icy fingers of terror tightening round his throat that he could at any moment plunge down to his death, so he prayed fervently to his Maker for urgent help.

At that moment he spotted far below the figure of an old, bent woman who held out her voluminous white apron and indicated to him that he should jump into it.

For some inexplicable reason, his instincts told him to trust her and he let his grip go, launching out towards her.

The apron did not hold him but broke his fall and when he came down it was not on some jagged rocks but in the cool, placid surface of the loch.

Gasping for air as he went under, suddenly he felt the old crone's wrinkled, bony hand pulling him out by the arms and found himself lying prone on the grassy bank, gasping for air and gazing up at her wrinkled but kindly old face silhouetted against the sky.

She grinned a toothless smile then croaked that he should go straight home and never go near the doves again, warning him that if he did, "The doonie will maybe no' be here to help ye again!"

She then vanished into thin air before he had a chance to thank her for saving his life.

There have been numerous tales over the centuries of doonies helping those in distress, like climbers or hillwalkers or daring fishermen, ever ready in lonely areas to lend a helping hand.

The Ghillie Dhu

THROUGHOUT THE 18TH CENTURY the good folk in the parish of Gairloch on the west coast of Ross and Cromarty knew of the nearby presence of a small, green, fairy sprite known as the Ghillie Dhu.

Despite his verdant colour, the name in Gaelic meant black servant and he was viewed as a friendly, guardian spirit. Few locals had actually come across him but one was a young girl called Jessie MacRae who had got lost out in the woods while picking flowers.

As darkness fell, she wandered around before collapsing into some shrubbery, bursting into tears. It was then that the tiny green man made his appearance beside her and asked why she was crying.

Gazing at the figure which seemed coated in green moss and fresh leaves and perched on a rock, she explained her plight.

He smiled and said he would lead her to safety and somehow she felt a strange reassurance in the presence of this unearthly being and followed him in the pale moonlight through the dark wood.

Sure enough, the welcoming lamps in her cottage were soon spotted through the drooping branches and, as her distraught parents ran out to greet her, Jessie waved a fond farewell to her uncanny helper as he retreated into the shadows of the night.

Years later the local laird, Sir Hector Mackenzie, a cruel despot, took it into his head to capture alive the Ghillie Dhu and put him on display in his dungeons, just to show what the aristocracy could do; and to this end he gathered together a posse of local farmers and gamekeepers. For a week they meticulously scoured the woods and moorlands, tirelessly beating their way through undergrowth in the birch woods, seeking their prey.

By now Jessie was grown up and, hearing of the hunt, made her way into the woods to warn her little green rescuer.

Keeping well ahead of the hunting party, she called out for the Ghillie Dhu to come to her and, as she leaned exhausted against a tree trunk, suddenly there he was, arms akimbo and laughing on a swaying branch.

When she warned him about the imminent danger of the search party, he reassured her that he knew what was happening and not to worry.

After another couple of days of thorough searching, the sweating hunters, baffled and finally fatigued, rested under the warm summer sun in a leafy glade.

They were then startled by a shrill whistle and high on a faraway ridge stood their quarry who waved his green cap at them, danced a merry jig then skipped away. He was never seen in the neighbourhood again but, a few days after the failed search, Sir Hector was found dead in his bed one morning from a heart attack, his open, staring eyes wide and frozen in horror.

The Man From the Sea

BIGHOUSE MANOR used to stand on the far northern coastline of Scotland beside the River Halladale where it ran into the sea and in 1802 the owner was an old, reclusive skinflint known locally as the Laird, a miser whose favourite pastime was counting the coins in the wooden chest he kept under his four poster bed.

One winter morning on a walk along the shoreline, he came across the body of a drowned seaman lying entangled in seaweed among the rocks, a not uncommon sight along that stormy coast.

Salmon fishermen soon appeared on the scene but none of them recognised the corpse and concluded he must have been washed ashore from some wreck.

The fishermen debated what to do and thought they should carry the corpse up to the nearest kirkyard and perform a decent Christian burial: but the Laird, who was still standing close by, baulked at this, believing he might have to contribute or maybe even pay entirely for the funeral arrangements. He persuaded the men it would be a lot simpler just to leave the body and let the tide wash it back out to sea and the dark depths where it could be swallowed up peaceably and, above all, cheaply enough.

The fishermen all had their daily tasks to be getting on with but nevertheless it was with some reluctance that they agreed to this line of action, hauling the body down to the lapping waves and covering it with some green seaweed like a verdant shroud.

Sure enough, when they returned this way in the evening twilight the tide had taken the body away into the wide bay and they thought no more about it.

But that night the Laird was awoken around midnight by a loud knocking at his main door and he crept downstairs in his nightshirt and cap, an old candle guttering in his fist.

Cautiously, he creaked open the strong, nail studded door which still had a stout chain restraining it so that he could peer through the gap to see who his visitor might be at this unearthly hour.

The Laird stood petrified and frozen to the spot for there, clearly in the silvery moonlight, stood the still dripping figure of the drowned man staring at him with glowing eyes burning redly with hate in the gloom, the damp apparition being garlanded in still dripping seaweed.

Slowly the corpse turned and silently strode away into the cold darkness. On looking down at the flagstones, the Laird saw that, where they should have been damp, they were instead completely dry.

Screaming in terror, the Laird ran upstairs to his bedroom, where he slammed shut the door and cowered under his bedclothes for the rest of the night.

The following day he fled the area, never to return and sold his property through the services of the nearest lawyer.

The Searcher

IN DECEMBER, 1777, there was a ferocious storm in the Pentland Firth which hit the whole northern coastline of Scotland and several vessels plying those heaving waters, both cargo and fishing boats, were smashed onto the rocks or swept onto the beaches.

Among them was a small coastal trading vessel which ran aground below the steep cliffs between Strathy and Portscerra in northern Sutherland.

The crew, desperately trying to get off, were all drowned in the mountainous waves as their craft was smashed to driftwood on the foaming reefs.

The only body found was that of the captain who was washed up high and dry on the beach, the corpse being found by some local salmon fishermen walking along the shoreline at dawn when the storm had calmed down.

Rifling through the dead man's pockets, they were surprised to find a considerable amount of gold coins; and, after a brief conference, they decided to keep this cash for themselves since they reckoned it did not belong to anybody else now and could be considered salvage, the latter being a substantial part of the local economy at the time.

However, they were concerned that if the death of the captain was officially reported to the authorities then their action might somehow be brought to light, so they decided to hide the corpse under some boulders along the beach; and that night they returned to the spot, carrying it up onto nearby moors where they hastily buried it under some peat.

From that time on, locals who were not in on the secret were mystified by the ghost of a sea captain regularly seen stalking the moors, a concerned look on his face as he seemed to be searching for something.

Years later, farmers cutting some peat on the moors uncovered a skeleton dressed in the threadbare uniform of a sea captain, brass buttons intact.

The bones were removed and given a proper Christian burial in the nearest kirkyard and thereafter the ghost was never seen again.

One of the fishermen, who originally found the body and stole from it, confessed on his deathbed to what he had done and revealed that all those involved had suffered terrible nightmares the rest of their lives after the incident, in which a grey, luminous sea captain seemed to be chasing them along a windy shore.

www.langsyneshop.co.uk
Scottish Books, Calendars, Gift Souvenirs and more

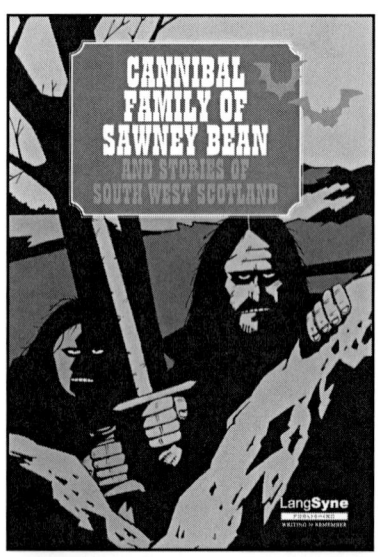

CANNIBAL FAMILY OF SAWNEY BEAN
AND STORIES OF SOUTH WEST SCOTLAND

Ghosts, Massacres And Horror Stories Of Scotland's Castles
by Margaret Campbell
Illustrations by John Mackay

Strange old Scots customs and superstitions

Strange Stories of Glasgow & the Clyde
Margaret Campbell

www.langsyneshop.co.uk